THE MARYLAND LINE CONFEDERATE SOLDIERS' HOME

AND CONFEDERATE VETERANS' ORGANIZATIONS IN MARYLAND

Daniel Carroll Toomey

Toomey Press
Baltimore, MD

Other titles by the author: *The Civil War in Maryland*
Marylanders at Gettysburg
Baltimore During the Civil War
Marylanders in Blue: The Artillery and the Cavalry

For information about this and other titles contact:
Toomey Press
P. O. Box 122
Linthicum, MD 21090
410-766-1211

Photographic Credits:
    D.C.T. Daniel Carroll Toomey
    All others indicated by specific source.

Book Design and Production:
    Cynthia Merrifield
    Merrifield Graphics and Publishing Service, Inc., Baltimore, MD

Printing:
    H. G. Roebuck & Son, Inc., Baltimore, MD

Library of Congress Card Control Number 2001130583
ISBN 1-929806-00-0

Contents

From the biographies of those who lived at the Soldiers Home in Pikesville.

"When I pitch my tent on the Eternal Camping Ground, I can truthfully say that I am proud that I was a Confederate Soldier and have no excuses to offer anyone."

Sydnor Bailey, Sergeant Major of the 40th Virginia Infantry

Introduction

Pikesville is a small town just inside the Beltway around Baltimore City. The main business district runs from Exit 20 east just over one mile to the Maryland National Guard Armory near the intersection of Slade Avenue. Both sides of Reisterstown Road are lined with shops and restaurants. Receding back from the modern day hustle and bustle are many quiet streets and big houses reflecting the Pikesville of old. In the center of this is a complex with an open arched entrance. A sign informs visitors that this is the Headquarters of the Maryland State Police. Near the curb a historic marker reveals the fact that these near-ancient walls once enclosed a Federal Arsenal and that later the same buildings were used as a home for Confederate veterans.

Few who pass by this grand old structure today reflect on the fact that this region was once the frontier of Colonial Maryland. The location of the old arsenal was a direct result of the War of 1812 and the Battle of Baltimore. For over forty years it was the Maryland Line Confederate Soldiers' Home. This is the story of the soldiers home and the old men with canes and crutches who did their last outpost duty at the entrance to the old arsenal, with a brief survey of Confederate veterans organizations in the state of Maryland. It was these organizations that founded the Soldiers' Home and cared for the old veterans until they were no more. It is their descendants that honor their memory today.

No man is an island and no one writes a history book by himself. In the preparation of this text I wish thank several people who contributed to the finished product. The first is Mrs. Mary Jane Kline for the use of her extensive file on the Pikesville Soldiers' Home. To Mrs. Virginia H. Sollers-Hoffmaster and Mrs. Donna Williams for their contribution to the chapter on the United Daughters of the Confederacy; and Mr. James Kurapka for the information he supplied on the Sons of Confederate Veterans. Finally I would like to express my sincere appreciation to my good friend Mr. Joseph Balkoski for his final review of the manuscript. Joe is an accomplished historian and an expert on the Maryland National Guard.

Figure 1.1 Roadside marker in front of Fort Garrison. (DCT)

Figure 1.2 Fort Garrison today showing ground level entrances. Originally access was by a retractable ladder to a door one story off the ground to prevent hostile Indians from gaining entrance. Also note the small square windows that allow for light and ventilation, and the safe firing of muskets when under attack. (DCT)

CHAPTER ONE

THE FOUNDING OF PIKESVILLE

The origins of Pikesville are steep in military tradition. During the late 1600's the colonial frontier of Maryland was only a few miles west of what is now Baltimore City. Settlers attempting to convert the wilderness into farmland needed protection from local Indian tribes such as the Susquehannocks, Senecas, and Delaware. The Colony organized a body of irregular troops known collectively as the Maryland Rangers to intercept Indian raids. These men were to be of good character and well versed in tracking and the use of firearms. They operated from small forts made of rock or logs and added the name of their general locale to the unit identification. Thus the Patapsco Rangers under the command of Colonel Neil Beall occupied a log fort between the Falls of the Patapsco River and Gwynn's Falls. Through this area the Seneca Trail traveled in a north-south direction.[1]

In 1692 Governor Coopley ordered three forts to be constructed along the Maryland frontier. One of these was built in present day Baltimore County near Pikesville and named Fort Garrison. It was located on a branch of the Jones Falls at the intersection of two major Indian trails, one used by the Senecas and one used by the Delawares. Built of stone, the fort measured approximately 48 feet long and 18 feet wide. Small windows a foot square or less surrounded the structure to allow for ventilation and lighting. The design also allowed for safe musket firing and at the same time prevented hostile Indians from forcing their way into the fort. Additional security measures included a steep stone roof to repel flaming arrows and no door at ground level. A retractable ladder left no easy access for attackers.

Known as the Garrison Rangers, soldiers from the fort patrolled an area that was approximately 70 square miles of total wilderness. Captain John Oldham was in charge of the fort and its nine-man garrison from 1696 to 1699. While commanding the fort, Captain Oldham obtained a patent for all the land surrounding the fort as well as the actual site of Fort Garrison. In 1699 he began to sell off portions of his property.

During the French and Indian War the fort was used as headquarters for Captain John Risteau, High Sheriff of the county. The fort still exists today—although altered with a ground level entrance and a second story. Possibly the oldest standing fortification in Maryland, it is listed on the National Register of Historic Places. Located off Stevenson Road, the 300-year-old fort is owned by Baltimore County.[2]

The founding force behind the town of Pikesville was a Baltimore City physician named James Smith. Doctor Smith was born in Elkton in 1771. He graduated from Dickinson College and studied medicine at the University of Pennsylvania. He later became known as the father of American vaccination due to his life-long interest in smallpox vaccines. Doctor Smith owned a tract of land along the Reisterstown Turnpike that included the site of the Burnt House Tavern erected in 1797. An unnamed community of some six or seven houses surrounded it.[3]

Here our story would have ended if it were not for the War of 1812. During the second conflict between the United States and Great Britain, Doctor Smith's friend, General Zebulon Montgomery Pike, was killed in the American assault on Little York (now Toronto, Canada) on April 27, 1813. Smith honored this brave general by naming the little town along the turnpike Pikesville.[4]

An equally important result of the war was that the British attacks on Washington and Baltimore proved to the federal government that military supply bases must be located far enough inland to prevent their capture or destruction by a hostile naval force. Pikesville, located on a major highway only eight miles from Baltimore, was one of ten sites chosen for the construction of an arsenal between 1816 and 1821. The others were Watertown, Watervliet, Rome, Frankford, Pittsburgh, Washington, Richmond, Augusta, and Baton Rouge. Of these only three, Albany, Baltimore, and Pittsburgh were to include a laboratory for the development of munitions.[5]

The government began negotiations soon after hostilities ended. During this time Dr. Smith sought to link his landholdings with the new military base as a means of promoting sales. On October 21, 1815, he placed an advertisement in the *Baltimore American & Commercial Daily*.

> "The following valuable Property (laid off as a town to be called "Pikesville" in honor of the late Gen. Z.M. Pike) is offered for sale in 200 equal shares or lots. It consists of the large Brick Tavern House, situated on Reisterstown Turnpike..., and 199 Vacant Lots laid off directly opposite The extensive buildings now erecting by the United States for an Arsenal and other public purposes....any Share or lot in this new village may be bought at the price of one hundred dollars..."

The government purchased 14 acres of land from Dr. Smith in June of 1816 for $895.00. When the deed was finally recorded on March 2, 1819, the town of Pikesville was officially put on the map as the site of a new arsenal.

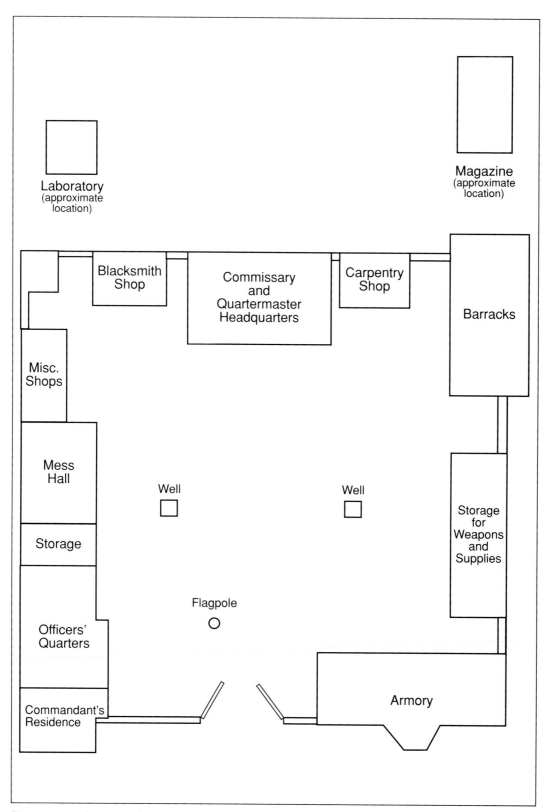

Figure 2-1 The United States Arsenal at Pikesville, Maryland, 1818–1880.

CHAPTER TWO

THE OLD ARSENAL

The establishment of the United States Arsenal and the transfer of land are somewhat confusing and will be restated for the ease of the reader. The Federal government approached Dr. James Smith in 1815 to buy the land. Construction was started in 1816 and took two years to complete. The deed finalizing the transaction was not recorded until March 2, 1819.

The first commander was Lt. Nehemiah Baden. A native of Maryland, Baden had served during the War of 1812 as an Assistant Deputy Commissary of Ordnance, a title that he exchanged in 1815 for First Lieutenant of Ordnance. He was later transferred to the Artillery, but retained command of the arsenal.[1]

On May 23, 1823, Lt. Baden, then a member of the Second U.S. Artillery, but still on duty with the Ordnance Department, wrote a report outlining the relationship of the arsenal to Baltimore City and the surrounding military region.

> "It was clearly perceived at the commencement of the late war with Great Britain that…Baltimore appears to have been particularly chosen as an object of attack…
>
> …Baltimore became the natural point for concentration of military forces for ulterior operations, and it was determined by the Government to erect an arsenal and depot somewhere in the rear of the city, to afford the facility of supplies to the forces operating in the immediate vicinity as well as those permanent military posts constructed for defense of this section of our frontier.
>
> This arsenal is situated on the Reisterstown Turnpike road, eight miles from the City of Baltimore. This road is smooth and firm at all seasons of the year, and affords the best land transportation: it

extends back north and west of the arsenal and passes through the upper counties of Maryland and into the productive counties of Pennsylvania and is a great land thoroughfare to Baltimore…The general aspect of the country around the arsenal is remarkable for its fertility of soil, gently rolling and well wooded, and is watered by Jones' and Gwynn's Falls… these advantages render it a proper position for an encampment of troops and of military supplies. The means by which stores are transported from this arsenal to the permanent posts intended to be supplied from it, are by hauling them to Baltimore, or the head of the navigable waters of the Severn River and from thence by water. The navigation of Patapsco is obstructed by ice a part of… December and January… The distance of this arsenal from Baltimore is eight miles, to Fort McHenry, eleven miles; to the head of the navigable waters of the Severn River, eighteen to twenty miles, and to Fort Severn in Annapolis, thirty-five miles."

Figure 2-2 The exploding bomb device on this corporal's collar denotes his service in the Ordnance Department. Enlisted men assigned to the Pikesville Arsenal before the Civil War would have worn a similar dress uniform when not on fatigue duty. (DCT)

Baden went on to state that the posts nearest the arsenal could be supplied in 3–4 hours and those on the interior line could be reached within 48 hours. This report underscores the importance of the arsenal to both national defense and the defense of the Maryland region in the years immediately following the war of 1812.[2]

The arsenal complex was completed at a cost of $84,044.31. It consisted of a number of brick buildings built in the Federalist style connected by an outer brick wall to form an enclosed compound with an arched entrance facing the Reisterstown Turnpike. The northeast corner of the perimeter wall contained a bell tower. The bell was rung every day at 8 AM, noon, and 6 PM. To the right of the entrance was the actual arsenal building. Centered in its front parapet was a stone panel containing the eagle emblem of the United States. To the left was the commanding officer quarters. This beautiful two-story structure was graced with intricate cast iron railings and ornamentation. Other structures included barracks, a laboratory and a stable. A powder magazine was also constructed with a double outer wall that was filled with water to prevent sparks from reaching its contents. Near the north wall was a small post cemetery containing less than ten graves. Two of these belonged to a Sergeant Smith and a Sergeant Corbett—both veterans of the Mexican War.[3]

The summer of 1831 saw the grounds of the normally tranquil arsenal rocked by a violent explosion that left one employee dead and another severely injured. Mr. Charles M. Lamberton of Carlisle, Pennsylvania, began his employment at the arsenal in 1825. On this particular day he and another man were working in the laboratory preparing fireworks that were to be sent to Annapolis for the upcoming Fourth of July celebration. Without warning there was an explosion that nearly demolished the laboratory building. When extracted from the debris the other man was found dead and Mr. Lamberton rendered deaf for the rest of his life. Despite his disability he continued to be employed at the arsenal as a clerk until 1875 when he suffered a sunstroke and was forced to retire after 50 years continuous service. The government granted him a half-pay pension until his death in 1881.[4]

In 1835 Lt. Baden was transferred to Florida and served in the Seminole Indian War. His replacement was another Maryland-born officer, First Lieutenant William Maynadier. His father was William Murray Maynadier a lieutenant of Cavalry during the War of 1812. Graduating third in the West Point class of 1823, he was commissioned a lieutenant of Artillery. Under Lt. Maynadier the arsenal became the center of social life in Pikesville. Dances were held between 1825 and 1840 and attended by the aristocracy of the neighborhood. At the same time he discharged his duties as a Regular Army officer. This included not only commanding the post, but also negotiating with civilian contractors in nearby Baltimore City, as the following letter will show.

Pikesville Arsenal, Md.
3rd march 1835

Gentn.

I send you herewith a copy of the rough draft of a 24 pdr. Iron Gun Carraige, which I showed you last Saturday. I then gave you the weights of different parts, which combine with the information you may be able to derive from this draft, will probably enable you to estimate the price at which you would be willing to contract for the manufacture of from 50 to 100 carriages. The draft (quarter size) exhibits a side view of one of the carriage, the thickness of metal being 3 inches. An additional thickness of metal may be required at the parts marked A&B to give the trunions of the gun and the axle of the carriage a greater bearing. The circular space at C will be required to be reamed to allow the free movement of roller D. The arms of wrought iron axles will be turned and the holes of the truck wheels reamed. Each carriage will require two of these checks which are to be connected by wrought iron transoms. Hoping that by this draft and the information you already possess, you may be able to make an estimate of the lowest price at which you can undertake to work and that you will inform me thereof.

> I am Genm, Respectfully
> Your obt. Servt.
> Wm. Maynadier
> Lt. U.S. Army

To Messre. Watchman & Bratt
Baltimore

Lt. Maynadier was promoted to captain in the Ordnance Department in 1838. His duties took him away from Pikesville. When the Civil War began he was promoted to Major and then Colonel and served as Inspector of Armories, Arsenals and Ordnance Depots. On March 13, 1865, he received the rank of Brevet Brigadier General. Continuing the family's military tradition his son, Henry E. Maynadier, received the rank of Brevet Major General.[5]

A different kind of conflict found its way to the arsenal in September of 1843 when Captain Charles May and Mr. Phillip Barton Key, son of Francis Scott Key, threatened to fight a duel over a lady residing in Baltimore City. On the 10th of September Sheriff Nicholas Tracy and Officer Fuller went to the arsenal with an arrest warrant from the county court to bring in Captain May in order to avert the duel. When the Sheriff attempted to arrest the man he thought to be Captain May, the gentleman asserted that he was not the subject of the *writ*. During the course of the conversation a dog came up to the man and Sheriff Tracy noticed "Capt. Charles May" engraved on its collar. With this circumstantial evidence the gentleman was forced to appear in court where it was discovered that he was the brother of Captain May. The duel was averted, but 16 years later Phillip Barton Key became part of a landmark decision when he was shot dead on the streets of Washington, DC, for having an affair with the wife of then Congressman Daniel E. Sickles. The future Union Army general then pled the first successful case of temporary insanity. His defense counsel was no other than Edwin M. Stanton.[6]

Figure 2-3 Captain Louis A. DeDarth Walbach commanded the Arsenal in 1849.

The post commander in 1849 was Captain Louis Augustus DeDarth Walbach. A member of the West Point Class of 1830, Walbach started his career in the Artillery before being transferred to the Ordnance Department. His promotion to captain came in 1848. On September 9, 1849 a new Catholic church was dedicated in Pikesville. Captain Walbach allowed the opening procession to begin from his home which was only 200 yards from the newly built St. Charles Borrome Church. In the procession were Archbishop Eccleston, Father White, the first pastor, numerous clergy and alterboys. After the ceremonies that included a Solemn High Mass, Captain Walbach invited the clergy back to his residence and served them dinner.[7]

Colonel Benjamin Huger of South Carolina was the last pre-Civil War commander of the arsenal serving from 1856 to 1861. Born in Charleston in 1805, Huger was appointed to West Point in 1821. He graduated eighth in the Class of 1825 and was commissioned a lieutenant in the Third Artillery. During the Mexican War he served on the staff of Winfield Scott as chief of both Ordnance and Artillery with the rank of captain.[8]

Receiving brevets of Major and Lt. Colonel, Huger returned from Mexico to resume the routine of a Regular soldier. In 1854 he was assigned to command the Pikesville Arsenal with the additional duty of inspecting United States foundries. His promotion to major came in 1855. Huger could never have imagined that his five

Figure 2-4 Colonel Benjamin Huger of South Carolina was the last pre-war commander of the Pikesville Arsenal. (DCT)

years of idyllic life among the cool shade trees of Pikesville and the glamorous society of nearby Baltimore City would be so quickly exchanged for an equal number of years of war and destruction that began in his native city of Charleston.[9]

On November 20, 1860, Secretary of War John B. Floyd ordered Huger to Charleston to assume command of the Federal arsenal there. His real purpose was to ascertain the military and political situation in that city as it related to the Federal Government's hold on the forts in Charleston harbor. After reporting to General Scott, Huger returned to Pikesville on December 15 and awaited future developments. He did not have long to wait. On Christmas Eve a telegram arrived from his brother, Cleland, urging him to accept a commission in the South Carolina state forces. Huger declined until secession was a fact. This is yet another example of a Regular Army officer not wishing to bring about a war and not able to fight against his native state if war came.[10]

The uncertainty lasted until April 12, 1861. When Huger learned of the firing on Fort Sumter, he submitted his resignation to the Adjutant General in Washington, DC. In a last ditch effort at peacemaker Huger offered his services to the state of Maryland. He was given command of the 53rd Regiment of Maryland Militia after the Pratt Street Riot when all of Maryland was under arms and expecting secession. Finally, on May 10, 1861, he placed the Master Armorer in charge of the Pikesville Arsenal and resigned his state commission. Major Huger then went to Richmond where he was commissioned a Major General on October 17, 1861.[11]

The Arsenal had a brief period of Confederate control in 1861 when it was occupied by a pro-Southern militia company. The Garrison Forrest Rangers, a throwback name from the colonial days, under the command of Captain Wilson C. Nicholas occupied the Pikesville Arsenal on March 28, 1861. Captain Nicholas, with the aid of First Lieutenant S. B. Mettam and 50 men armed with muskets, held the Arsenal until mid-May. When General Benjamin F. Butler occupied Baltimore on May 13, Federal troops were sent out from the city, forcing the Rangers to disband and reoccupying the arsenal.[12]

During the war years the arsenal grounds were primarily used as a training center for Union Volunteer regiments. The Purnell Legion was organized here between October and December of 1861. Regiments from other states were also stationed at the arsenal. At the end of the Civil War the Pikesville Arsenal reverted back to the Federal control. In 1866 Captain Michael J. Grealish, a Military Store Keeper in the Ordnance Department, assumed command of the post on June 1. When he was transferred to Atlanta in 1875, the duty of caretaker fell to Sergeant Alfred Guther. Guther was the last member of the Regular Army to command the post.[13]

The face of the nation had changed drastically since 1816 and Pikesville was a long way from the current American frontier. This combined with a vast change in weapons technology made the old arsenal obsolete. Congress authorized the transfer of both land and buildings as an outright gift to the state

List of Stores &c Remaining at Pikesville Arsenal Md. on the 31st June 1861.

	Articles		Articles
5	Gunners Callipers. (3 Extra)	1	Bridle (very old)
5	do Quadrants.	5	Bell stands (wood very old & useless)
1	Port-fire Clippers.	1	Bell
1	Pistol Bullet Mould.	1	Cart (Hand do nearly worn out.)
1	Fife	1	Cultivator (Hand do (Extra).
1	Gun Block.	1	Harrow (Hand do (Extra)
3	Sling Cart chains.	2	Ladders
1	Gun rampart (incomplete)	1	Half Bush: Measure (old)
20	Files assorted	1	Peck do (old)
23	pcs cast steel	2	Ploughs (+ extra (not very good)
10	Bees Wax.	1	Spirit Level.
1	Sets Alphabets.	1	Safe Iron (useless)
3	Felling Axes	7	Stoves.
2	Leifs for Rocket Moulds.	2	Garrison Flags.
28	Port-fire Leifs.		
1	Fire Engine.	1	Storm do.
30	" Buckets	1	Set Halyards (worn out nearly)
24	Shot Gauges.	1	Roller for Walks &c (Extra)
200 ft	Leading Hose.	1	Wood " " for Land (")
1	Copper Kettle.	1	Cart Harness. (old ").
12	Powder Measures.	100.000	Musket Flints.
3	Copper Mealing Pans.		
4	Port-fire Leifs relieves.	150.000	Rifle Flints.
2	Suction Hose joints.		
1	Copper. Scoop.		
1	" Skimmer.	25.000	Pistol Flints.
7	Turners Tools.	1529	pds Hay (Mixed.)
1	" Lathe	3	Wheel-Barrows. (almost useless.)
1	Anvil	1	Gun now in use by the

1 Bellows
1 Work Bench.
1 Mill Saw (circular)
50 ft Belting for Saw.
1 Pallet Knife.

Troops at this place. The Comd: Officer here wishes to use it for a short time, as the one issued to the comp. is undergoing Repairs.

Figure 2-5 List of supplies and equipment on hand at the Pikesville Arsenal as of June 11, 1861. The quantity of rifle and pistol flints indicated the obsolete nature of its purpose. (DCT)

11

of Maryland for use by its military forces or any other purpose it might deem appropriate. The State Legislature approved the offer and officially accepted the gift on June 29, 1880.[14]

State Adjutant General J. Wesley Watkins appointed Daniel A. Fenton to the position of Caretaker. Fenton had served during the war as First Sergeant in Company G of the Second Maryland Infantry CSA. He was replaced two years later by Samuel B. Mettam who remained in charge of the post until its conversion to the soldiers' home.[15]

Figure 2-6 Roadside marker in front of the Pikesville Arsenal. (DCT)

Figure 2-7 Interior view of arsenal parade ground. (Booth)

Figure 3-1 The Maryland Line Confederate Soldiers' Home, 1894. (Booth)

Figure 3-2 View from inside the front gate of the Soldiers' Home. (Booth)

CHAPTER 3

THE MARYLAND LINE CONFEDERATE SOLDIERS' HOME

In the decades following the Civil War one of the most common scenes in American society was the veteran. All too often his badge of honor was an empty sleeve, a cane, or a crutch. Twenty years after the fighting had ended, age began to be a factor in their condition as well. All had not been mere boys at the time of their enlistment. The dual burden of age and war wounds left many unable to support themselves. An ever-increasing number would also need a final resting-place as well. The Union veterans had a decided advantage over their old adversaries. The federal government provided them with pensions, veterans' homes, and national cemeteries. The Confederate veteran was cared for by state-run programs and numerous benevolent organizations, but a popular slogan of the time said it best—"The Pensions of the Confederate Soldiers abide only in the hearts of the people."

Maryland's divided loyalties during the war yielded two separate groups of veterans. The Union Volunteers of 1861–1865 were cared for by the federal government. Its Confederate veterans were cared for by two organizations unique to the state. The first was The Society of the Army and Navy of the Confederate States in Maryland. One of its stated goals was to "…aid those veterans in need of shelter or any other form of assistance." The other was The Association of the Maryland Line. While its original purpose was to preserve the history of Maryland units serving in the Confederate Army, it eventually took the leading role in caring for the veterans.[1]

These two organizations joined forces to hold the Confederate Relief Bazaar of Maryland at one of the Maryland National Guard armories on April 7–11, 1885. A total of $31,000 was realized from the event. This money was in turn invested in a 25-year annuity that yielded $2,200 per annum for the care and burial of the veterans. A very considerable sum for its day, this amount fell short of the amount needed to keep up with the ever-increasing number of men in need. Consideration was first given to the building of a cottage at the Home for Confederate Veterans in Richmond, specifically reserved for residents of Maryland. This plan was soon abandoned in favor of an application to the state government for the use of the property known as the Pikesville Arsenal as a home for Maryland Confederate Veterans. A bill quickly passed in the State Legislature in February of 1888 making the Association of the Maryland Line the custodian of the property and appropriating $5,000 annually for the repair and maintenance of the buildings.[2]

When the Association of the Maryland Line acquired control of the old arsenal, Pikesville was little more than a village composed of about two dozen houses and a population of 250 people. There were two general stores, Corbett's and Foley's, Emmick's harness shop, Fields drugstore, Davis's blacksmith shop and Lowery's Saloon. The main attraction before the soldiers' home opened was the Sudbrook House—a getaway spot for residents of Baltimore City to escape the summer heat.[3]

There was much work to be done before anyone could take up residency. From the time the state took possession of the arsenal until its transfer to the Association, no practical use was made of the property and no repairs were made to the buildings by the state or federal government for a period of 20 years. Renovations began in April of 1888. In only two months enough progress had been made to allow for the official dedication of The Maryland Line Confederate Soldiers' Home which took place on June 27. The Hon. George W. Brown, Mayor of Baltimore in 1861, presided. Other notable attendees were Gen. A.H. Colquitt, U.S. Senator from Georgia; Gen. Charles E. Hooker, Congressman from Mississippi; Hon. Frederick C. Latrobe, Mayor of Baltimore City; Gen. Bradley T. Johnson; and many others.[4]

The Maryland Line Confederate Soldiers' Home was administered by the Board of Managers specifically appointed by the governing body of the Association of the Maryland Line. This board was chaired for many years by James R. Wheeler, a well-known Baltimore banker and veteran of Co. E, First Maryland Cavalry. The Board of Managers was aided in no small way by a Board of Visitors. Many of the women in this group were active in the United Daughters of the Confederacy. Virtually a "who's who" of Maryland Confederate women, the board's first president was Mrs. Bradley T. Johnson. Under her direction committees were established for each month of the year and it was the duty of each committee member to visit the home at least once during their designated month. The chairperson of these committees would then submit a written report on the care and condition of the veterans that was in turn sent to the Board of Managers. Despite this overwhelming collection of bureaucracy, it is obvious that the comfort of the aging veterans was the ultimate goal of all concerned.[5]

The home opened with seven men in residence. They would soon be joined by many others. As each new arrival approached the front archway they were greeted by a rainbow shaped sign declaring their new residence to be The Maryland Line Confederate Soldiers' Home. Suspended from the center of the sign was a giant Botonee or Maryland Cross – the symbol of Maryland service in the Confederate Army. Within the walls of the old arsenal all the major buildings had been converted for their specific use. Other than honoring the immortal Stonewall Jackson, each building was named for a Maryland Admiral or General. Many of the rooms within these buildings were furnished by family members or veterans groups as memorials to those lost during the war.[6]

ADMIRAL FRANKLIN BUCHANAN BUILDING

Named for the Confederacy's first admiral, Buchanan commanded the ironclad *Virginia* at Hampton Roads in 1862 and the *Tennessee* at Mobile Bay in 1864. It contained four rooms.

"The Ridgely Brown Room" was named for the commander of the First Maryland Cavalry who was killed at South Anna, Virginia, on June 1, 1864. Furnished through the efforts of Mrs. John F. Hunter, it contained four beds and accompanying furniture. On the wall were a picture of Lt. Col. Brown and a copy of General Order No. 26 issued by then Colonel Bradley T. Johnson announcing Brown's death.

"The Gill Room" was furnished by Mr. John Gill in the memory of his brother, Sommerville P. Gill, who was killed at Pegram's Farm, Virginia, while serving in Company A of the Second Maryland Infantry. The room contained four beds made of cherry wood with accompanying wardrobes, tables, lamps, and rockers. It also contained a stove and a large rug to improve the comforts of its occupants.

"The Jenkins Room" was furnished by George Jenkins in memory of his brother John who was a member of the Maryland Guards, Twenty-first Virginia Infantry. The room contained two beds and had its own fireplace.

So strong was the attachment of the men who served in Captain William H. Murray's companies of the First and Second Maryland Infantry that after the war they formed their own association. These men furnished the four-bed "Murray Room" in honor of their captain who had been killed at Gettysburg on July 3, 1863. On the wall hung a photograph of Murray and one of the association's monument at Loudon Park Cemetery.

BRIGADIER GENERAL HENRY LITTLE BUILDING

General Little was killed while in command of a division at the battle of Iuka, Mississippi, in March of 1862. It contained nine memorial rooms.

"The Baltimore Light Artillery Room" was furnished by survivors of the battery in memory of their fallen comrades. It contained two beds and associated items of furniture required for a comfortable stay.

"The Chantilly Room" was one of the few private rooms at the home. Mrs. H. F. Goring furnished the room and named it for the plantation "Chantilly" where the First Maryland Infantry was stationed in the fall of 1861.

"The William E. Colston Room" was one of the first rooms opened at the home. This two-bed room was furnished by Captain Frederick M. Colston in memory of his brother who was killed in Mosby's attack on the Cole's Cavalry camp on Maryland Heights January 10, 1864.

C. Ridgely Goodwin furnished "The Goodwin Room" in memory of his brother who was only 17 years old when he died at Gettysburg. He enlisted in the Oglethorpe Light Infantry in April of 1861. The room contained beds and furniture for two men.

Located in the building that also bore his name, "The General Henry Little Room" was furnished by General Little's widow. The room contained two oak beds. The pillows were stuffed with feathers from game shot by the general. On the walls hung portraits of Generals Lee and Jackson, and the prints entitled "The Charge of the First Maryland Regiment" and "The Prayer in Stonewall Jackson's Camp."

Mrs. William Reed dedicated "The McKim Room to the memory of her brother Robert who was a member of the Rockbridge Artillery. He was only 18 years old when killed at Winchester, Virginia, on May 25, 1862.

Colonel Charles Marshall, a member of General Lee's staff and a distinguished lawyer in Maryland after the war, furnished "The Marshall Room" in honor of his two brothers who were killed during the war. They were Robert I.T. Marshall of the Washington Artillery and James M. Marshall of the Fourth Virginia "Black Horse" Cavalry. The room contained two beds.

"The Stonebreaker Room" was dedicated to the memory of Edward L. Stonebreaker who served in Company C, First Maryland Cavalry by his brother Joseph. Joseph R. Stonebreaker was the author of *A Rebel of 61*.

Mrs. Martin B. Brown elegantly furnished "The Virginia Room" in honor of the Old Dominion State. There were two beds made of walnut. The china wash bowls were inscribed "Virginia" in gold gilt.

BRIGADIER GENERAL LLOYD TILGHMAN BUILDING

This West Point graduate gallantly held Fort Henry with only 100 men while the rest of the Confederate force was transferred to Fort Donelson. He was killed at Champion's Hill on May 16, 1863. At the time of its opening this building held the carpenter's shop and the paint shop.

BRIGADIER GENERAL JAMES J. ARCHER BUILDING

Born in Hartford County, Archer entered Confederate service as colonel of the Fifth Texas regiment. Promoted to Brigadier General in June of 1862 he fought in every battle of the Army of Northern Virginia until captured at Gettysburg on July 1, 1863. One of the "Immortal 600" he remained in captivity for a year. When exchanged he was in poor health and died in October of 1864. On the first floor of the building was the "Raleigh C. Thomas Memorial Hall." On the second floor was a storeroom and sleeping quarters for employees of the home.

Figure 3-3 The Raleigh C. Thomas Memorial Hall and Library. (Booth)

"The Raleigh C. Thomas Memorial Hall" was the home's library. A spacious room, it measured 50 X 27 feet. It was furnished with oak tables, chairs, and rockers. The shelves contained 1,000 books donated by friends of the home from all over the state. In addition to this reading material about 100 different newspapers were sent regularly at no charge. The family and friends of Raleigh Thomas donated $1,000 to the project in the memory of this veteran of the First Maryland Cavalry.

ADMIRAL RAPHEL SEMMES BUILDING
The most famous raider of the Confederate States Navy, Semmes commanded the *Sumter* and the *Alabama* capturing or sinking 80 vessels. When Richmond was evacuated in 1864, he commanded a brigade of naval personnel thus becoming the only officer during the Civil War to hold the rank of admiral and general. It contained two memorial rooms.

The Brewers Exchange of Baltimore furnished "The General Robert E. Lee Room" as a token of their admiration for the high ideals and strong character that General Lee possessed. Its purpose is not known.

"The Warfield Room" was dedicated to the memory of two brothers, Albert G. and Gassaway W. Warfield both of whom served in Company A of the First Maryland Cavalry. Their grandfather was Colonel Gassaway Watkins Warfield who fought in the Revolutionary War and was the last serving officer of the original Maryland Line.

MAJOR GENERAL ARNOLD ELZEY BUILDING
A Regular Army officer at the outbreak of the war, Elzey was the first colonel of the First Maryland Infantry Regiment C.S.A. He took command of a

brigade at First Manassas. Seriously wounded at Gaines' Mills in 1862, he was given command of the Defenses of Richmond. At the end of the war Elzey was serving as Chief of Artillery in the Army of the Tennessee. This building contained the Office of the Superintendent, Quartermaster Room, Pharmacy, and Surgeon's Office.

Besides the usual office furniture, the walls of the Superintendent's Office were decorated with numerous prints and documents of historic importance. Among the framed items were a Muster Roll of Company H, First Maryland Infantry and one of Company D, First Maryland Cavalry. There was also a print of Camp Saint Mary's where the Maryland Line wintered in 1864.

In the Quartermaster's Room one side was lined with shelves to hold the bed linens. The other side contained bins and boxes of consumable items issued to the residents as needed. One such item was their uniform. Another, considered far more important, was tobacco.

The Surgeon's Office was located on the east side of the Elzey Building. Here the old soldiers came on their Sick Call. The doctor on duty would tend to their needs and prescribe different remedies. Dental care was also given in this building.

The "E. Kirby Smith Room" was actually the home's pharmacy. It was furnished by Mrs. Decatur Miller in the highest possible style. The floor was carpeted. The walls were of hand carved oak with a matching medical case. Lighting was provided by a brass chandelier. Mrs. Miller requested the room be named in honor of General Smith, who although not a Marylander, was an outstanding officer and surrendered the last Confederate army on May 26, 1865.

BRIGADIER GENERAL CHARLES S. WINDER BUILDING

Charles Winder was one of many Maryland-born West Pointers who chose to serve the Southern cause. He was present at the firing on Fort Sumter. After First Manassas he was given command of the Stonewall Brigade and participated in the Valley Campaign and Seven Days battles. Winder was killed by artillery fire at the battle of Cedar Mountain in August of 1862.

The Winder Building contained the Dining Room, Commissary Department and Kitchen. The Dining Room measured 48 X 18 feet. In it were four large oak tables and matching chairs. The room was kept in order by a detail consisting of a sergeant and five men. This room was furnished by Lt. George W. Wood, a pre-war resident of Louisiana. The Commissary Department consisted of two small rooms. The kitchen was located near the dining area.

BRIGADIER GENERAL WILLIAM W. MACKALL BUILDING

General Mackall served on the staff of General Albert Sydney Johnson in 1862 and was Chief of Artillery for General Joseph E. Johnson in 1864. Between these two assignments he commanded troops in the field with distinction. Mackall's name was given to the Superintendent's house. It was the

Figure 3-4 Four large oak tables accommodated the veterans in the Dining Room. (Booth)

building just to the left of the front entrance. It is a two-story brick structure of the Federalist period with a full basement. A six-foot wide porch graced the front of both levels with fine wrought iron and woodwork.

STONEWALL JACKSON INFIRMARY

This was the only building not named for a Marylander. From the formation of the Confederate army at Harpers Ferry in 1861 until his death, Jackson had a long association with the First Maryland Infantry and the many Marylanders who served on his staff and in his Second Corps. The laboratory that had been

Figure 3-5 The old Powder Magazine was converted into the Stonewall Jackson Infirmary. (Booth)

the scene of the fatal explosion in 1831 was chosen to be the home's hospital building. Originally located 100 yards from the main complex as a safety precaution, its isolation was also appropriate for those who were severely ill. This four-bed facility was furnished by a number of ladies.

MAJOR GENERAL ISAAC R. TRIMBLE BUILDING

Although born in Virginia, Trimble took up residence in Maryland 30 years before the war and after the war until his death. A West Point graduate, he worked as an engineer building railroads in the West Indies, New England, and Maryland. He lost a leg at Gettysburg while leading Pender's Division in "Pickett's Charge." The Trimble building is perhaps the most important structure in Pikesville. It is the old arsenal building to the right of the main entrance. It contained five memorial rooms and "The Relic Hall."

The "Richard B. Buck Room" was furnished by his widow. Buck served as a lieutenant in the Seventeenth Virginia Infantry. It contained four oak beds, rockers, and other items of comfort including a china wash bowl.

The "First Maryland Artillery Room" was furnished by Lt. Col. Richard Snowden Andrews, the unit's first commanding officer. Its contents are unknown.

Harry Gilmor enlisted as a private in Turner Ashby's Cavalry in 1861. By 1864 he commanded his own battalion of Maryland Cavalry and took part in the famous Johnson-Gilmor Raid through Baltimore County in 1864. The "Lt. Col. Harry Gilmor Room" was furnished by the surviving members of his command—The Second Maryland Cavalry.

The "Frank H. Sanderson Room" was furnished by his brother, William Cook Sanderson. Frank Sanderson was a member of Murray's Company A,

Figure 3-6 Two old soldiers sit comfortably in the Gilmor Room—one of the many rooms furnished by organizations or private individuals and named for a Confederate soldier. (Booth)

Second Maryland Infantry. He died on July 4, 1863, from wounds received the previous day on Culp's Hill. A portrait of Sanderson hung on the wall in this room with a memorial plaque beneath containing his service record.

The "Zollinger Memorial Room" was dedicated to the memories of Lt. William P. Zollinger and his brother Jacob E. Zollinger. Both men served in the Second Maryland Infantry. Jacob died of wounds received during the fighting on Culp's Hill. The room was furnished through a collaboration of Mrs. Charles A. Oakford, Mrs. W. G. Power, and Mrs. William P. Zollinger.

The most sacred place within the walls of the old arsenal was a room on the first floor of the Trimble Building simply called "The Relic Hall." The main hall was about 100 feet long. The walls, ceiling, and center support beams were all painted white and there was an ample supply of sturdy wooden chairs. Numerous prints, paintings, and flags adorned the walls. Glass cases held swords, uniforms and other war relics. One of the favorite items there was a camp chair used by Robert E. Lee that visitors took pleasure in sitting in!

In this room, formal ceremonies and indoor social events were held. It was also the repository for a collection of Confederate memorabilia that few states North or South could rival in its day. That an institution in an non-seceding state would be the custodian of so many artifacts relating to the icons of the Confederacy and momentous events during its four-year existence bears testimony to the value of the service rendered by the Maryland men who enlisted in that cause. Its value today, both historically and financially, may well be incomprehensible.

Figure 3-7 The "Relic Hall" was located on the first floor of the old arsenal building. It contained hundreds of items related to the South's struggle for independence. (Booth)

To dramatize this statement the author has chosen ten items from the nearly 500 known to have been part of this once great collection. A complete list of The Relic Hall's holding will be found in Appendix B.

Robert E. Lee's Headquarters Battle Flag
J.E.B. Stuart's Commission as Major General
Coat worn by Gen. Turner Ashby when killed in 1862
Battle Flag of the First Maryland Cavalry
Log Book of the CSS *Shenandoah*
Last Confederate Flag to fly over Fort Sumter
John Brown's Spy Glass
Adm. Franklin Buchanan's Frock Coat
Battle Flag of Pegram's Artillery Battalion[7]

Two buildings deep into the courtyard and to the left of the center walkway was a 125 foot flag staff painted white from which flew "Old Glory" and not the "Stars and Bars" although many such flags could be found elsewhere on the premises. The flagstaff was erected at the considerable sum of $500.00, a portion of which was paid for by James R. Wheeler, Chairman of the Managers. It would have been the focal point for many outdoor ceremonies. A second flagstaff was later erected in the center of the parade grounds. It was struck by lightning on October 1, 1913, and completely shattered. It was never replaced.[8]

The home was run along the lines of a military installation, the only mission of which was the care and comfort of its soldiers. To that aim the rules were few and as mild as possible. In fact there were only five.

1. Uniforms must be worn on Sundays, holidays, and all other occasions when the Superintendent may direct.
2. No member of the Home will be permitted to leave the grounds unless by the consent of the Superintendent.
3. Use of liquors especially prohibited, unless by Surgeon's order.
4. Quarreling and boisterous behavior are strictly prohibited.
5. Any complaints from the members of the Home shall be in writing, and forwarded through the Superintendent to the Board of Managers.

The management and staff of the Home in 1894 consisted of the following individuals.

Superintendent . . . . .William H. Pope
Surgeon . . . . .Dr. W.P.E. Wyse
Pharmacist . . . . .Dr. Benjamin Gough
Dentist . . . . .Dr. B.R. Jennings
Adjutant . . . . .Charles W. Semmes
Quartermaster . . . . .William H. Davis

Figure 3-8 A group of old Rebels pose at the base of the flag pole. All but one are in their uniforms supplied by the Home for Sundays and special events. (DCT)

Commissary . . . . .Richard C. Briscoe
Inspector . . . . .B. R. Jennings
Librarian . . . . .Matthew Green[9]

The Home opened with seven residents. One of these was Solomon A. Gephard who, like several others, chose to reside at Pikesville even though he had a wife and family. He lived until 1904, which might indicate that poor health was not the reason for his choice of residence. By the end of the year the population had grown to 28 of whom 2 died and 4 were dismissed. While some men did enter the Home in poor physical condition as the early deaths indicate, others were in their 40's and 50's and still able to perform light duty. Those that were able were assigned jobs tending the garden, milking cows, working in the kitchen and mess hall or aiding in the medical offices. A few worked at odd jobs around the town as long as they were able.

Notification of assembly and details was communicated to the veterans by the ringing of an iron bell in front of the Winder Building.

Sick Call	2 Bells
General Detail	3 Bells
Vegetable Detail	4 Bells
Laundry Detail	5 Bells
Assembly	6 Bells

Reduced to working in the Library or Quartermaster Department after years of combat experience, they were still old soldiers at heart. Some would get drunk at Lowery's Saloon or get into fistfights over real or imagined transgressions. For breaking the rules, Superintendent would order them off the premises. When this happened the residents of Pikesville would take them into their homes until they could negotiate their return. One such offender was Billy Donahue who was called "The Scout." Mr. Cox, the owner of Milford Mill, would allow Billy to stay in a cabin on his millpond until the Superintendent "cooled off."[10]

While the $5,000 contributed by the State Legislature was a significant portion of the Home's yearly budget, additional money was needed to care for the veterans whose population reached over 150 at its peak. Donations by Confederate Veterans organizations, the United Daughters of the Confederacy, and private individuals were also required to keep the Home running smoothly. One fundraiser that entailed considerable pomp and ceremony was the annual Jousting Tournament, Festival and Ball that was held in conjunction with Defenders Day, every September 12 from 1893 to 1913. Announcements were sent out and programs printed, listing the Knights attending and rules of competition.[11]

A second annual event that affected the lives of the residents was Confederate Memorial Day. Each year on June 6, special services were held on "Confederate Hill" at Loudon Park Cemetery. All those that were able put on

Maryland Line Confederate Soldiers Home.

BOARD OF GOVERNORS.

JAMES R. WHEELER,
JAMES L. AUBREY,
R. JAMES STINSON,
HUGH McWILLIAMS,
DANIEL L. THOMAS,
MARK O. SHRIVER,
D. RIDGELY HOWARD,
FRANK T. BLAKE.

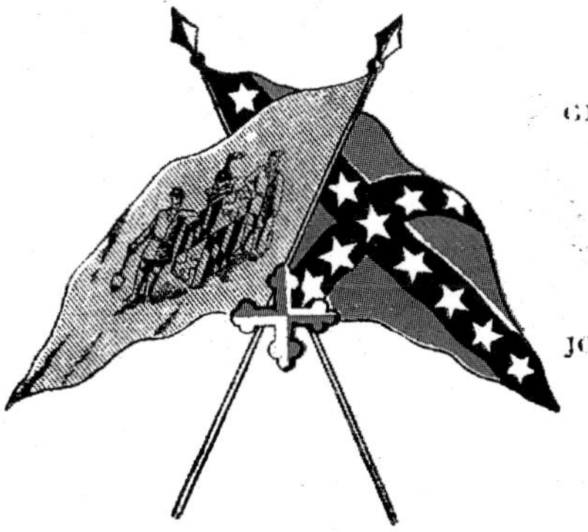

BOARD OF GOVERNORS.

GENL. BRADLEY T. JOHNSON,
PRESIDENT.
CAPT. GEO. W. BOOTH,
SECRETARY.
DANIEL L. THOMAS,
TREASURER.
JOHN F. HAYDEN,
CAPT. GEO. R. GAITHER,
AUGUST SIMON,
CAPT. WM. L. RITTER.

BOARD OF MANAGERS.

JAMES R. WHEELER, CHAIRMAN,
EX-OFFICIO, GENL. B. T. JOHNSON,
CAPT. GEO. R. GAITHER,
CAPT. GEO. W. BOOTH,
AUGUST SIMON,
DAN'L L. THOMAS.

Superintendent,
WILLIAM H. POPE.

Surgeon,
DR. W. P. E. WYSE.

Pikesville, Md., August 16th, 1899.

Dear Sir:

The Managers of the Maryland Line Confederate Soldiers Home beg to announce they will hold their annual Tournament, Festival and Ball at the Home, Pikesville, Md., on Maryland Day, Tuesday, September 12, 1899. The program will be of an interesting character, and the proceeds devoted to the maintenance of the Home. We hope you will bear in mind that this is one of our main supports.

Contributions of supplies, such as eatables, candies, fruit, cigars, etc., for sale at tables, will be most gratefully received. Send to—

JAMES R. WHEELER,
Commonwealth Bank.

AUGUST SIMON,
208 North Howard Street.

G. F. MASSON,
3 West Pratt Street.

CHAS. ANDREWS,
Meat Stall, 95 Lexington Market.

PIKESVILLE EXPRESS,
Hand House, N. Paca Street.

BAGGAGE ROOM,
W. M. R. R., Hillen Station.

Admission to Ground, - -	FREE
Admission to Tournament, - -	10 Cents.
Reserved Seats, - - - -	25 Cents.

Enclosed please find tickets. Kindly disposed of them and remit proceeds to

W. H. POPE, Superintendent,
or any of the Board of Managers.

Figure 3-9 Announcement for the annual jousting tournament and ball held every year on Defenders Day. This was the Home's major fundraiser from 1893 to 1913. (DCT)

their gray uniforms and were taken to Loudon Park were they marched in tribute to their fallen comrades. In 1910, 68 old soldiers under the command of Captain R. J. Stinson made the trip.[12]

As the years stretched out into the next century many of these old soldiers made their final journey to "Confederate Hill" or one of the other cemeteries around Baltimore City in a streetcar named "Delores." This was a Baltimore & Northern passenger car converted to a funeral car with a side-loading door for the coffin that allowed the deceased and his mourners to travel as a unit. A funeral party could rent the "Delores" with its motor man and a conductor for a fee of only $20.00.[13]

One of the veterans whose passing could not go without notice was John Francis Key. A private in the First Maryland Infantry, he was the grandson of Francis Scott Key, author of the *Star-Spangled Banner*. Key entered Pikesville on July 3, 1894. He died at the age of 92 and was at that time the oldest living resident at the Home.

Time had an effect on the administrative staff of the Home as well as its residence. Dr. Wright resigned in 1891 and was replaced by Dr. William P. E. Wyse as post surgeon. Superintendent Pope died in December of 1904. His replacement was Mr. R. J. Stinson, whose death in turn caused the appointment of Mr. William H. Todd. Todd also died in office and was replaced by Mr. Lamar Holliday who was the first of his position to manage a resignation. The last Superintendent of the Maryland Line Confederate Soldiers' Home was Theophilus Tunis, himself a veteran of the First Maryland Cavalry. Tunis assumed his duties in September of 1925 and died in September of 1932. At the time of his death there were only two veterans remaining at Pikesville—Hobart Aisquith and Henry Atzerodt. These two men literally outlived the Home that cared for them. No longer practical to operate a facility for so small a population, these two surviving veterans were moved to private residences in Baltimore City. Their expenses were paid for by the State of Maryland. Asquith was the last survivor of the Pikesville Home. He died at City Hospital on August 16, 1937 after injuring his leg in a fall.[14]

The old arsenal remained in limbo until 1937 when the State Legislature passed a bill giving administration of the property to the Veterans Memorial Commission that consisted of nine members. On April 29, 1938, Mrs. Tunis, the widow of the Home's last Superintendent, moved out. The next day Colonel Edgar Hobbs, a veteran of World War One, moved in as custodian of the property. A major portion of the arsenal complex was given to the 110th Field Artillery, Maryland National Guard. Mr. Matthew M. Tunis, son of the last Superintendent, was given the position of Caretaker. It was a small world.[15]

The declining population during the later years of the Soldiers' Home had caused a surplus of buildings that were expensive to maintain. The stable and Stonewall Jackson Infirmary had been torn down. The old magazine was in poor condition. The long, low building known as the Dormitory was turned over to a ladies organization around 1921. They renovated the building and operated the Pikesville Health Center for over 20 years. During World War II Miss Ruby B.

Revere was the nurse in charge. In 1934 Boy Scout Troop #353 was granted use of the Commissary Building as their headquarters and meeting place. They in turn made all necessary repairs to the building.

Following the outbreak of World War II, Baltimore Chapter No. 1 of the American Red Cross was granted use of the Administration Building for the production of war supplies. Reminiscent of the Ladies' Aid Societies of the Civil War, they prepared "kits" for the boys at the front. They also sent books, magazines, and other items to boost the morale of the American GI.[16]

In 1939 the Pikesville Arsenal was selected by the U.S. Department of the Interior for historic preservation. A statement by the Secretary of the Interior Harold L. Ickes read in part "...known as the Old United States Arsenal... has been selected by Advisory Committee of the Historic American Buildings Survey, as possessing exceptional historic or architectural interest and being worthy of the most careful preservation for the benefit of future generations..."

During World War II the Maryland State Police made their headquarters at the Pikesville Military Reservation. With peace came the return of the 29th Division and the State Police needed a new home. Colonel Beverly Ober, then the Superintendent of the State Police, made the suggestion that the nearby site of the Maryland Line Confederate Soldiers' Home be acquired as the new home for the State Police headquarters.

Rehabilitation began in 1949. Only three of the original buildings belonging to the Pikesville Arsenal and the perimeter wall were still in existence. The State Police would use the commanding officer's residence and the arsenal building. Great effort was taken to maintain the historic integrity of these building while at the same time converting them to modern usage. The venerable old arsenal building that once held the "Relic Hall" is now designated Building "A" and houses Legal Council, Internal Affairs, Planning and Research, and the Volunteers in Police Service departments. Ownership of the Powder Magazine had been transferred to the Kiwanis Club of Pikesville in 1950. This same year the Quartermaster Division, Motor Pool, Executive, Field, and Communications offices were relocated to their new home. On September 9, 1950, dedication ceremonies were held. The former United States Arsenal and Maryland Line Confederate Soldiers' Home was officially the Headquarters of the Maryland State Police.

Additional buildings constructed within the walls during the 1950's were designed to be compatible with the original structures. In the center of the parade ground the Fallen Hero's Monument was placed opposite the entrance to Building "C" which houses Personnel and Training. Dedicated on December 5, 1989, it contains, at the time of this publication, the names of 38 members of the Maryland State Police force that have died in the line of duty beginning with Officer John W. Jeffrey, September 1, 1921. In 1994 The Maryland State Police Alumni opened a museum on the first floor of the building that was originally the Superintendent's residence. It contains an excellent collection of uniforms, weapons, and other memorabilia related to the Maryland State Police, which began operations in 1921.[17]

Figure 3-10A One of only three original buildings surviving today, the Commandant's Residence now contains a museum dedicated to the history of the Maryland State Police. (DCT)

Figure 3-10B The old Arsenal Building still proudly displays the eagle emblem of the United States in its center parapet. (DCT)

Figure 3-10C The Powder Magazine is located to the right and rear of the enclosed complex. The Kiwanis Club of Pikesville acquired ownership in 1950. (DCT)

Figure 3-10D The old looks out onto the new. A view of the front gates from inside the Arsenal's walls as a car passes on Reisterstown Road. (DCT)

Charles Aloysious Donnelly.

Born at Emmitsburg, Frederick Co. Maryland. — Enlisted April 1861. at Charleston, S. Ca, in Co. C "Confederate States (Regulars) Infantry. for the term of War. served in Castle Pinckney. Charleston, Fort Sumpter, James Island, Stone River, &c, taken Prisoner at Fisher's Hill. Va. June 1864. sent to Camp Morton, Indiana, released in April 1865.

Patrick Duggan.

Born in Ireland Age 75 years, Enlisted Spring of 1861. at Staunton, Va, in Co B. 7" Va Infantry. — Same year detailed as ward Master at the Staunton Va. Military Hospital, C. S. A. where I remained until the end of the War.

George Freeman Darden

Enlisted as Private in Co. K. 31st N. C. Regt. of Infty. A. D. 1862 at Charleston S. C. Discharged from the Confederate Army in 1865 at Ft. Delaware. Was at that time 2nd Lieutenant. My occupation is watch maker and I am 70, years old.

Figure 4-1 Copy of page from biographical sketchbook. (DCT)

CHAPTER 4

BIOGRAPHICAL SKETCHES OF THE MEMBERS OF "MARYLAND LINE" CONFEDERATE SOLDIERS' HOME JANUARY 1900

To this point our story has primarily covered the history of the buildings that comprised the Federal Arsenal and the Maryland Line Confederate Soldiers' Home at Pikesville. The real story lies with the old soldiers who actually lived out their final days within those protective brick walls. The seven men that entered the Home in 1880 were the vanguard of old Rebels that would total over 460 during the next 44 years. Most of them had served in the Confederate army. A handful were naval veterans and at least two were from the Secret Service. Their predominant rank had been private with some representing every rank from drummer boy to full colonel. The highest-ranking veteran was Brigadier General Lucius B. Northrop. During the war Northrop was the Commissary General of the Confederacy. He entered the Home in poor health on April 18, 1893, at the age of 82 and died in February of 1894.[1]

The youngest men to enter the Pikesville Home were only 46 – the oldest were 90. Most were in their 60's and 70's. Surprising, many did not stay. About 20 were dismissed or otherwise "Dropped from the rolls" for various infractions.

Over 60 chose to leave on their own volition, going to live with family or friends as the opportunity presented itself. These men were considered "Discharged." Two others simply packed their things and left without giving notice. The last man to enter the Home was Private John H. Waters. He was 90 years old and a veteran of Company E, First Maryland Cavalry. His stay would be a brief one. Entering on July 1, 1931, he passed away in December of the same year.[2]

For obvious reasons, some form of criteria had to be established to control the number of men accepted into the home. Only one of the following requirements needed to be meet by an applicant to considered for admittance:

1. Was a citizen of Maryland when the war began.
2. If not a citizen of the state, served in a Maryland command during the war.
3. Acquired legal citizenship in the state of Maryland after the war and retained the same at their time of application.
4. Citizens of Washington, DC, were eligible for admission due to the special relationship between Maryland and the District of Columbia.[3]

Along with their application were usually one or more letters of recommendation, often by noted Confederate officers, explaining their worthiness for acceptance. To complete the application package a series of questions were asked concerning their military history.

Name?
When and where born?
When and where enlisted?
Company, Regiment, and term of service?
If re-enlisted same information?
If taken prisoner when and where and how long in captivity?
If wounded in action when and where?
If paroled when and where?
Any special event during the war you were a witness to or part of?[4]

While this information was requested in a standardized format, the responses were recorded in more or less a conversational style. In 1900 someone had the idea to sort these information sheets alphabetically and transcribe them into a ledger book. The book has a marbleized cover and measures 8 inches by 13 inches with alphabetized tabs and 300 numbered pages. There are 212 biographical sketches in the ledger book. This is just under half of all those who resided at the Pikesville Soldiers' Home. It is believed that this project was begun in 1900 and for some reason never completed. The latest recording is for Private Thomas H. Snowden who entered the Home on January 5, 1909.

It is obvious from the handwriting that three different people actually did the transcription. Unfortunately their names do not appear anywhere to give them credit for their service rendered. A clue to one of these individuals identity is a notation at the end of one of the biographies signed D. M. Key. This in all probability was Daniel Murray Key, one of the residents of the home. The following is the first ever transcription of these soldiers' personal histories. Only a minimum amount of punctuation has been introduced to allow for their thoughts to be understood and no attempt has been made to research their facts and dates. They did not have the luxury of the OR's on CD ROM and the Internet when they made their statements 20 or more years after the war.[5]

Now the reader is invited to sit back and in his mind's eye take a streetcar ride to Pikesville. Get off the car and walk through the main entrance where a giant Maryland Cross hangs from the sign declaring this the Maryland Line Confederate Soldiers' Home. As you walk along the main sidewalk past the old arsenal building, you meet small groups of old men with long beards in gray uniforms—it's Sunday. Some have crutches or they are in wheelchairs. Nearly all of the others walk with a cane. Sit with them. Ask them their name. In what regiment did you serve? Did you ever see Robert E. Lee? Were you at the battle of…?

JOHN GROVE ADAM

Born at Alexandria, VA, March 10, 1840. Enlisted April 1861 at Alexandria as a private in Company A, Seventeenth Virginia Infantry for the war. Transferred to Company D, Fourth Virginia Cavalry spring of 1863. Taken prisoner at Battle of Malvern Hill 1862. At Point Lookout, MD, for 9 weeks. Exchanged. Again captured the day before Lee's surrender. Confined at Farmville, VA, two weeks then paroled. Was in the following Battles: Bull Run, 2nd Manassas, Williamsburg, Seven Pines, Gettysburg and all skirmishes my command took part. Slightly wounded in both legs at Raccoon Ford latter part of 1863 in the fight between Gen. Fitz Lee and Gen. Pleasanton.

JACOB ABRISCH

Born in Prussia, August 17, 1825. Enlisted at Lancaster C.H., VA, April 1861 in Company D, Fortieth Virginia Infantry Regiment for the war. Discharged by Col. Brockenborough on account of eyesight. Never a prisoner. Never wounded. Was in but one engagement, the First Battle of Fredericksburg, VA.

GEORGE WASHINGTON ALDRIDGE

Born February 28, 1842, in Prince Georges County, MD. Enlisted as private in Company C, First South Carolina Infantry at Charleston on March 1861 for one year. Re-enlisted March 1862 at Wilmington, NC, in Co. F, Third North Carolina Infantry. In which command I remained during the rest of the war. Wounded at

Gettysburg July 2, 1863. Made a prisoner on retreat from there. Incarcerated at Fort Delaware for 23 months. Paroled & released from there June 1865. Engaged in the battles of Gaines' Mill, Malvern Hill, Second Manassas, South Mountain, Sharpsburg , Fredericksburg, Chancellorsville, and Gettysburg.

SHANNON FLETCHER BUTTS

Born at Lewisburg, VA, in 1839. Enlisted C. S. service September 1863 as Chaplain in Forty-second Virginia Regiment Infantry at Orange C.H., VA. Left the service June 1865 near Salem, VA.

JOSEPH WILLIAM BRIGHTWELL

Born in Louisa County, VA. Enlisted Co. B, Second Maryland Cavalry, Col. Harry Gilmor, at Richmond for 3 years or the war on the 7th Day of September 1863. Was in every Battle or Skirmish of the command to close of War. Received a slight wound on right arm at New Hope Church, VA. Left at the disbandment of the command after surrender of General Lee.

JOHN BROWN

Born in County Waterford, Ireland. Enlisted April 1861 at New Orleans, LA, in Company A, Wheat's Battalion "La. Tigers." Term of service expired September 1862. Re-enlisted September 13, 1862, at Winchester, VA, in Company E, Second Maryland Infantry. Wounded at 1st Manassas in leg by fragment of shell. Wounded and arm broken by minie ball charge at Culp's Hill, "Gettysburg." Wounded at 2nd Cold Harbor in same arm by fragment of shell. Wounded at Squirrel Level Road in right shoulder by minie ball. Taken prisoner at Gettysburg. Taken to West Building, Baltimore, MD. Sent to City Point, VA, and Paroled. In all Battles and actions in which my command was engaged and never in the Guardhouse. Served until the close of the war.

JAMES HENRY BURNHAM

Born at Baltimore City. Enlisted at New Orleans, LA, as a private in Company D, First Louisiana Infantry. Transferred to Company I, First Kentucky Infantry in 1863. Transferred to Company B, Thirty-fifth. Virginia Cavalry (Col. Elijah White). Wounded in leg at Dranesville, VA, 1861 by minie ball while in First Kentucky. Taken Prisoner near Leesburg, VA, 1863. Taken to Fort McHenry, MD. Then to Point Lookout, MD. Exchanged March 1865. In Battles of Knoxville, TN, Fair Oaks, VA. Gettysburg, PA and other actions.

JOHN L. BRISCOE

Born in Jefferson County, VA. Enlisted February 1861 at Raymond, Hinds County, MS, as private in what afterwards became Company C, Twelfth Regular Mississippi Volunteer Infantry which was organized at Corinth, MS, on the 20th of April 1861 and reached the Army of Northern Virginia the later part of July 1861. Was promoted as captain and Q.M. and assigned to duty at Maj. Gen.

R. H. Anderson's Head Quarters in September 1862. Was with the Army of Northern Virginia from July 1861 until the surrender of General Lee's Army at Appomattox C.H. on Sunday Morning April 9, 1865.

WILLIAM BYER

Born in Germany. Was naturalized a citizen of the United State in Baltimore before the war. Left Baltimore to join the Confederate Service. Enlisted May 1861 at Harpers Ferry as private. Was honorably discharged in August 1862 at Gordonsville, VA. Time of service having expired. On account of being crippled in the leg, could not enlist in the Regular Army. I then enlisted in Company G, First Regiment of Richmond Defenders Captain Ruddick, in whose command I served until the end of the war. Was in the following named battles: First Manassas, Front Royal, Harrisonburg, Cross Keys, Port Republic, Rappahannock Bridge, Gaines Mills, Malvern Hill, Winchester, and a number of skirmishes.

THOMAS HEWLINGS STOCTON BOYD

Born Montgomery County, MD. Enlisted April 1861 at New Orleans, LA, as ensign in Company I, First Louisiana Infantry. Was made Commissary of the Regiment until April 1862. On the 19th of April 1862 was transferred to Read's Heavy Artillery with a commission as First Lieutenant. Was commissioned Lt. colonel of the Forty-seventh Battalion Virginia Cavalry operating in South Western Virginia. Was wounded in the left leg at Gaines' Mills, VA. Received a bayonet wound in my side at Bristoe Station, VA. Left Richmond April 2, 1865, in charge of special car, in the same train that carried President Davis and his family. Saw the last interview between President Davis, his cabinet, and General Lee. Was paroled at Danville, VA, April 15, 1865.

WILLIAM ROBERT BYERS

Born in Cambridge, Dorchester County, MD. Enlisted June 1861 at Tappahannock, VA, as a private in Company H, Forty-seventh Virginia Infantry. Was discharged, time of service having expired, June 1862. Re-enlisted in June 1862 at Richmond, as second lieutenant Company E, Second Maryland Infantry. Was afterwards promoted to First Lieutenant. Was taken prisoner at Hatcher's Run April 2, 1865. Was sent to Johnson's Island and released in June 1865. Was wounded in the leg by a musket ball at Winchester, VA. Was wounded in the left side by a fragment of a shell at Pegram's Farm. Was in the following battles: Seven Pines, Gaines' Mills, Williamsburg, and all other battles and skirmishes in which my command was engaged.

GEORGE WASHINGTON BARRETT

Born in Baltimore City. Enlisted May 1, 1861, as private in Company H, Third Virginia Infantry. Was taken prisoner at Five Forks, April 1865. Sent to Point Lookout, MD, and released in June 1865. Was in all the battles and skirmishes in which my command was engaged.

JAMES EDWARD BRIDDELL

Born in Snow Hill, MD. Enlisted for one year July 1861 as private in Company B, Thirty-ninth Virginia Infantry. Was honorably discharged, time of service having expired, in November 1862. Re-enlisted in November 1862 as private in Company G, Second Maryland Infantry. Was in all the battles and skirmishes my command was engaged in. Was wounded in the left leg above the knee in the charge on Culp's Hill, at the battle of Gettysburg. Was taken prisoner on the field and sent to the West Building Prison (Hospital) in Baltimore, MD. There to Chester, PA, and from there to Point Look Out, MD. Was released in June 1865.

THOMAS JEFFERSON BROWN

Born in Philadelphia, PA. Moved to Richmond, VA, while quite young. Enlisted May 11, 1861, at Richmond, VA, as a private in Hampden's Artillery. Afterwards transferred to Pickett's Division and promoted to corporal. Was in all the battles and skirmishes my battery was engaged in. Received a wound in the shoulder from a musket ball in front of Petersburg, VA. Was in the hospital at the time of the surrender. In business in Baltimore, MD, for past twenty years.

HENRY RICHARD BONN

Born in Baltimore, MD. Enlisted May 1861 at Richmond, VA, for one year as private in Company H, First Virginia Infantry. Was honorably discharged, time of service having expired, May 1862. Re-enlisted May 18, 1862, at Richmond, VA, as first sergeant in Company A, Twenty-fifth Battalion Virginia Infantry. Was in all the battles my command engaged in. Never took the Oath, was not paroled.

ARTHUR BRIZENDINE

Born in Essex County, VA. Enlisted May 21, 1861, at Tappahannock, VA, as a private in Company A, Fifty-fifth Virginia Infantry. Was in the following named battles: Seven Days battles around Richmond, continuing until June 26. Cedar Mountain, Second Manassas, three engagements, Chantilly, Harpers Ferry, Sharpsburg, Blunt's Mill, Fredericksburg, Chancellorsville, Mine Run, Wilderness, Spotsylvania, Shady Grove Church, Bathesda Church, Cold Harbor, Weldon Railroad and Peebles' Farm. Was severely wounded in the abdomen by musket ball at Peebles' Farm September 30, 1864. Was reported mortally wounded. Was confined to my bed for six months. Was paroled at Richmond, VA, May 1865.

HEZEKIAH HENRY BEAN, M.D.

Born in Charles County, MD. Enlisted June 15, 1861, at Richmond, VA, as lieutenant in Company I, First Maryland Infantry. Was wounded severely in the foot by a minie ball at the Battle of Cross Keys, VA. Discharged June 15, 1862, at Staunton, VA, term of services expired. Was in all the battles in which my command was engaged.

John Philip Brehm

Born in Germany. Enlisted August 1862 as private Company I, First Maryland Cavalry for the war. Prisoner August 1864. Captured on the Potomac River and sent to Fort McHenry. Then to Baltimore City Jail. Then sent to Fort Delaware. Exchanged from latter place January 1862. Again a prisoner at Battle of Weldon Railroad and taken to Point Lookout, MD. Discharged June 1865. (Wounded) Participated in battles of Fisher Hill, VA, Gettysburg, PA, West Virginia raid and other engagements.

John Boyce

Born at Baltimore, MD, August 2, 1840. Enlisted February 1861 at Charleston, SC, in Company G, First South Carolina Infantry for one year. Re-enlisted in same company and Regiment 1862 for 3 years or the war. Wounded in Fort Sumter by fragment of shell in 1863. Wounded in leg on Morris Island by minnie ball. Participated in Battle of Fort Sumter and the siege of same. On Morris Island was Chief Gunner when the Ironsides was driven from Fort Moultrie. Was on Sullivan's Island. Served to close of war.

Sydnor Bailey

Born in Westmorland County, VA, on January 28, 1844. Enlisted 21st day of May 1861, at Lancaster County, VA, in the "Lancaster Gray's." When the Fortieth Virginia Infantry Regiment was formed in June 1861, was made quartermaster of the regiment and continued in that position until the Seven Days Battles in front of Richmond when I was ordered back to my company and took part in all the engagements around Richmond. At Second Manassas was taken with Typhoid Fever. Sent to Chimborazo Hospital and remained there until after the First Maryland Campaign, when I rejoined the regiment. Was made sergeant major. Took part in all the battles of the Army of Northern Virginia. At the battle of Gettysburg was wounded in the head in the third day fight—"Pickett's Charge," but was only absent long enough to have my head bandaged by the Surgeon, Dr. Newton, who was afterwards Bishop Newton of Episcopal Church in Virginia.

Col. Brockenborough who commanded the brigade and myself were the last men to cross the Potomac River on Pontoon Bridge at Falling Waters after Gen. Pettigrew was killed. Continued with the regiment in all the battles and skirmishes until the end finally came. Was captured at Sailor's Creek when generals Ewell and G.W.C. Lee were trying to reach the Army of Northern Virginia under Gen. R. E. Lee. On our way to City Point Lieut. Blackward, Pvt. Cundiff and myself made our escape by bribing a Negro Soldier, giving to him my silver watch. We tried to join Gen. R. E. Lee, but before we could reach him we were re-captured and paroled after the surrender of Gen. R. E. Lee. After that I came to Baltimore and followed the occupation of traveling salesman. When finally my health broke down I came to the Maryland Line Confederate Soldiers' Home at Pikesville.

When I pitch my tent on the Eternal Camping Ground, I can truthfully say that I am proud that I was a Confederate Soldier and have no excuses to offer anyone.

MARTIN BLUEFORD BROWN

Born at Shevino, Culpeper County, VA, January 8, 1846. Enlisted at Harpers Ferry on April 20, 1861, in Brandy Rifles, Captain Stockton Heath, Thirteenth Virginia Infantry, Col. A. P. Hill. In October or November the company was reorganized when I joined Black Horse Cavalry, Fourth Virginia Regiment and served as a private until the surrender. I carried first dispatch in army riding from Winchester to Culpeper Court House the night of April 18, 1861. Sent by Major John Ambler to Governor Letcher stating that Harpers Ferry was captured and burned. Returned night of April 19. Joined company at Harpers Ferry. Surrendered when Lee surrendered at Appomattox Court House.

GEORGE HENRY BROWN

Was born January 9, 1831, in Frederick, MD. Left home in 1863 and went to Richmond where I enlisted as private in Arsenal Battalion in which command I remained until the fall of Richmond when I was taken prisoner and remained there until Gen. Robert E. Lee surrendered when I was released and came direct to Baltimore, MD. Wounded by a spent ball in the groin at Fort Harrison July 20, 1863, which was only a slight wound.

THOMAS JEFFERSON BARTHOLOMEW

Born at Nashville, TN, April 10, 1842. Enlisted as corporal in Company E, Seventh Tennessee Infantry in Sumbler County, TN, April 1, 1861. Served in this command 3 years and 6 months when I was detailed as a harness maker in the Ordnance Department, Richmond, where I remained until the surrender of Gen. Robert E. Lee at Appomattox. Was in all the battles that my command engaged in. Never was captured. Wounded two different times. Both times flesh wounds caused by shells of enemy bursting. First time wounded was at Battle of Seven Pines, VA, Sunday afternoon and sent to Chimborazo Hospital Richmond. The second time wounded was at Cedar Mountain, VA, August 9, 1862. Was sent this time to No. 9 Exchange Hospital Richmond. When well returned to command again.

HARRIS CHAMBERLAIN BLANCHARD

Born On Park Avenue, Baltimore, MD, July 22, 1844. Enlisted as a private in Loudoun County Virginia, June 6, 1864 in Company F, Forty-third Regiment Virginia Cavalry, Mosby's command. Was promoted to sergeant. Remained in this command till expiration of war. When General Lee surrendered the command was disbanded. Took Oath of Allegiance to U.S. at Harpers Ferry in 1865. Never captured. Never wounded.

JAMES LUTHER CASTLE

Enlisted October 5, 1862, as private in Company C, Second Maryland Infantry. Born in Frederick County, MD. Wounded at Gettysburg in the Capture of Culp's Hill. Received the wound in the breast by a minnie ball. Again wounded June 3, 1864, at Cold Harbor in the head by a minnie. Captured about 5 miles from Petersburg during our retreat, April 5, 1865. Sent as a prisoner to Heart's Island, NY. Released June 1865. In the following named battles: Cold Harbor, Weldon Railroad, Hatchet's Run, White Oak Swamp, Petersburg, Winchester, VA and Gettysburg. When wounded at Gettysburg was sent to Fort McHenry. Thence to Fort Delaware and Point Lookout. Exchanged from latter place December 25, 1863.

JOSEPH FRANCIS CRYER

Born in Saint Mary's County, MD, May 1, 1825. Enlisted June 15, 1861, as private Company F, Fortieth Virginia Infantry Regiment. Engaged in the following battles, Bull Run, Seven Days, fight in front of Richmond, Cedar Mountain, Culpeper Court House, Chancellorsville, in the latter engagement I received a ball in my shoulder which paralyzed my right arm. Discharged in 1864 disability.

WILLIAM AUGUST COALE

Born in Anne Arundel County, MD. Enlisted as private in First Maryland Artillery, July 28, 1861, at Richmond. Wounded at Malvern Hill in shoulder by fragment of shell. Discharged December 1864 on account of wound. On duty at Maryland Hospital until after the close of the war. Engaged in the following battles: Williamsburg, Fredericksburg (twice), Chancellorsville, Winchester (2), and all other engagements in which my command was engaged.

PATRICK CONNOLLY

Born in "Lough," Ireland. A citizen of Baltimore, MD, in 1861. Entered service December 1861 as a private Company E, First South Carolina Infantry, at Charleston, S.C. Promoted to sergeant. Wounded at Cold Harbor in the hand by a piece of shell. Also in the left leg by a minnie ball. Paroled at Wilmington, NC, April 1865.

HENRY DEWITT CLINTON

Born in Baltimore, MD. Enlisted September 1862 at Sheperdstown, VA, as private in Company K, First Virginia Cavalry. Was transferred to Company K, Second Maryland Cavalry in 1864. Was wounded in the shoulder by a pistol ball, at Westminster, MD, and taken prisoner. Was confined in Fort McHenry. Was transferred to Fort Delaware, and from there exchanged after about one month imprisonment. Being wounded was detailed to Arsenal Guard of Richmond. Remained in the service until the war was over.

WILLIAM CONLEY

Born in Baltimore County, MD. Enlisted June 5, 1861, at Norfolk, VA, as a private in the Baltimore Heavy Artillery for one year. At the expiration of the year was discharged. On the 14th of June 1862, re-enlisted in Company G, White's Battalion of Cavalry. Was taken Prisoner at Bunker Hill, VA, January 3, 1863. Was first confined at Camp Chase, OH. The transferred to Fort Delaware from which prison I was released June 23, 1865. Received a wound in the hip from a musket ball at Mount Jackson, VA. Was in the battle of Seven Pines and others in which my command was engaged.

JOHN EDWARD CHAMBERS

Born in Baltimore City. Enlisted February 1861, in Baltimore City as private in Company D, First South Carolina Artillery. Was promoted to corporal, then to sergeant. Was wounded in the hand at Fort Moultrie by the premature discharge of a gun. Was engaged in the attack on Fort Anderson and the Floating Battery. The battles of Poeataligo and the battery supported by Shaw and his Negro command. Engaged in the capture of the Gunboat Isare Smith, and the recovery of the guns of the USS *Keokuk* sunk in the action off April 7, 1863, off Fort Sumter for which latter services I received a reward of fifty dollars in money and a furlough of 15 days. Was transferred to the Baltimore Light Artillery in July of 1863 as a private. Was paroled at Lynchburg, VA, April 13, 1865.

FENTON BLACKWELL CLABAUGH

Born at Hancock, Washington County, MD. Resided in Cumberland, Allegheny County, MD, until 1859. Then went South in the employment of the Adams Express Company where I was when the war began. Enlisted about December 1861 at Manassas Junction, VA, as a private in Company C, First Maryland Infantry. Was honorably discharged May 17, 1862. The company's service having expired. Was in General Winder's office for some months. Then with General Gardner who was in command around Richmond. Then worked on the erection of the defenses around the Weldon, NC, at which time I was made Post Adjutant and remained there for nearly two years. Was in the engagements of Black Water, Boone's Mills, and other points in North Carolina in which my command took part. In the engagement at Boone's Mills was knocked from my horse and wounded in the face by a saber blow. Was never taken prisoner. Was paroled at Charlotte, NC.

DANIEL RICHARD DENNY CHEEZUM

Born in Caroline County, MD. Enlisted in October 1862 at Austin, TX, as a private in Bee's Artillery. Remained with my command until disbanded in May of 1865 at Houston, Texas.

JOSEPH ALOYSIUS CAHILL

Born in Youngstown, PA, during the temporary residence of my parents there. Their home being at Cumberland, MD, and my ancestors being residents of the state of Maryland from 1632. Crossed the river at Cumberland with my gripsack in my hand unmolested by hundreds of Yankee soldiers sitting on the banks of the river. Walked to Springfield, VA. From there went to Romney in a wagon, and from there by the regular mail stage to Winchester where I enlisted about the 20th of August 1861 as a private in Company F, Seventh Virginia Cavalry. Was in the following named battles: Romney twice, Blue Gap, Winchester, Kernstown, Fishers Hill, and all the battles and skirmishes my command was engaged in until the time of transfer to the Quarter Master Department where I was at the time of the surrender of General Lee. Was paroled at New Market, VA.

JOHN CAVANAGH

Born in County Tipperary, Ireland. Enlisted in early part of 1861, in the state of Mississippi, Company I, Pettitt's Rifles, Seventeenth Mississippi Regiment for the war. In the latter part of 1862 was detailed to work in Tredegar Iron Works in Richmond. At the same time I was enrolled in a Virginia Regiment to do guard duty at Prisons in Richmond. In battles of First Manassas, Ball's Bluff, Seven Days battles in front of Richmond, and all other actions whilst with my command. Was at the Tredegar Works when General R.E. Lee surrendered.

JAMES THOMAS COTTINGHAM

Born at Baltimore City September 30, 1842. Enlisted 1862 at Macon, Georgia, as a private in Company A, Fifth Georgia Battalion. Was made first lieutenant of said company three months after enlistment. Was in the different engagements from Knoxville, TN, to Atlanta, and from the latter to Franklin, TN. Then to Columbia, SC and up to Greensboro, NC. Surrendered there on April 23, 1865. Once slightly wounded and never a prisoner. After surrender attempted to join Gen. Kirby Smith's Trans-Mississippi Department, but halted at Fort Valley, GA, upon learning of the capture of President Jefferson Davis.

WILLIAM HENRY CONOWAY

Born at Baltimore City November 6, 1833, Enlisted February 16, 1861, in Charleston, SC, as a private in Company C, First South Carolina Regulars for one year. Re-enlisted in Richmond in Company B, Thirty-fifth Battalion Virginia Cavalry. Participated in the capture of Fort Sumter, Battles of Wilderness, Second Fredericksburg, and in several raids with my command and all other engagements that the Battalion was in. never wounded and never a prisoner. Paroled in Loudon County, Virginia, May 1865.

WILLIAM RENIE COYNER

Born 24th day of July, 1840, at Leadsville, Randolph County, VA. Enlisted at McKenzie, TN, April 21, 1861, in Company E, First Kentucky Infantry. Mustered in at Nashville, TN, under Colonel Blanton Duncan. Term of service 12 months. Came on to Virginia and landed at Harpers Ferry. Stationed on

Maryland Heights until evacuated. Fell back to Bunker Hill, then to Winchester. From there to Manassas Junction. Got there too late for the battle. Was at the storming and capture of Munson's Hill. In the fight on the 21st of December 61, at Drainsville. Helped to save the cannon and was complimented very highly by my captain for so doing. Went into Winter Quarters until the army fell back to Richmond. Thence on to Yorktown. Placed in trenches to support Howitzer No. 3 of Richmond. In trenches on the 18th of April, 1862, when we fought Brook's Vermonters and whipped them back. Evacuated trenches and fell back to Williamsburg. Had a skirmish there and drove Yanks back. Covered retreat to Richmond and then went into Camp Lee where we were mustered out of the service. Being non-residents of the Confederate States, remained in Richmond until after Seven Pines fight. Went in to that fight with Rodes Brigade May 31, 1862. In the skirmish June 1st, 1862. Left Richmond for the Valley of Virginia. Then to West Virginia. Scouted with McNeal for 2 months. Then joined the First Virginia Cavalry Company E, Captain McLung. In all the battles until December 20, 1862. Transferred to F Company, Seventh Virginia Cavalry, Captain Key Kenall. On scouting duty until Jones Raid. In fight at Greenland Gap, Fairmont, Bridgeport, them back to the Valley at Brandy Station and Upperville. Then on to Gettysburg. Fought at Fairfield, and complimented by both my lieutenant and captain. In fight at Emmitsburg and gap this side. In all the night fighting on the Blue Ridge trying to save wagon trains. In fights at Hagerstown and Funkstown and below in all of them until we fell back across the Potomac and then back to Brandy Station. In fight at the latter place all day. Fell back to Rapidan River. In fight at Jack's Shop. Got furlough October 2, 1863, to recruit men in West Virginia. Was captured by the Fourteenth West Virginia Infantry October 12, 1863. Taken to Fort McHenry, Baltimore, MD. Placed in cell and tried by Military Court Martial for recruiting inside lines against Articles of War #54 issued December1861. Found guilty and sentenced to hard labor during the war. Transferred May 12, 1864, to Fort Delaware. Placed to work, but refused to do the same. Then confined in a cell for 12 hours. Took me out and placed me in the officers' barracks until June 12, 1865, when I was released. Whole time of imprisonment 20 months.

ROBERT BOWIE CHEW

Born in Calvert County, MD, October 11, 1842. Enlisted September 8, 1862, Frederick County, MD, as private in First Maryland Battery of Artillery for the war. Engaged at Harpers Ferry September 12, 1862, Sharpsburg September 17, 1862, Boteler's Ford September 19, 1862, Fredericksburg December 13, 1862, Fredericksburg second battle 1863, Winchester and Stephenson's Deport 13-14&15 of June 1863, Bristoe Station in the endeavor to cut off Meade from Washington, DC, Mine Run November 27 or 29,1863, Tottopottomoy Creek 1864, Turkey Ridge 1864, Cold Harbor 1864, Siege of Petersburg June 15 to December 24, 1864. Engaged in 1865 at Dutch Gap, Sailor's Creek and Appomattox. Promoted to sergeant during the siege of Petersburg. Surrendered at Appomattox Court House April 9, 1865. Arriving in Washington, DC, after surrender, was imprisoned at Alexandria, VA, for about one week. Wounded at Stephenson's Depot June 15, 1863, a bullet having passed through my right arm.

MICHAEL RICHARD CLARK

Born in Baltimore on September 29, 1835. Enlisted for one year as private in Purcell's Battery of Artillery about June 26, 1862, (General Field's Brigade) where I remained until my time of service expired. At the expiration of the year of my enlistment was laid up in hospital in Richmond. When Captain Pegram, my old captain visited me and advised me not to again enlist as I was in no condition for active service.

PATRICK HENRY COYLE

Born in Ireland year and date I don't remember. Enlisted as private April 1861 in Company D, Captain James Herbert First Maryland Infantry at Harpers Ferry. In which command I remained until the regiment was disbanded in the summer of 1862. Never re-enlisted. Never wounded or taken a prisoner.

WILLIAM HENRY CAHILL

Born November 14, 1846, near Emmitsburg, Frederick County, MD. Enlisted as private in the Confederate States Army at Winchester August 15, 1861, in Company F, Seventh Virginia Cavalry on the term of one year. Re-enlisted in camp near Harrisburg at the end of the term in same Company, same Regiment for three years or during the war. Never was taken prisoner and never paroled.

Was in two different battles at Romney, Hampshire County, VA. The first on October 1861. The other in the spring of 1862. Also in the engagement of Kernstown 1862, Trevilian Station, Cedar Creek and in cavalry skirmish in numbers beyond my power to recollect. Was wounded in cavalry skirmish at Honeyville, Page County, VA, June 19, 1863. Gunshot wound through right elbow joint, which was resected in hospital at Charlottesville. After which I served as clerk to Major Robert Saunders, Quartermaster of Virginia, until May 1864. From then until the fall of Richmond April 2, 1865, in the office of Quartermaster General. Not being near my company was never discharged, but left Richmond and went South to New Orleans, LA.

JAMES MOSHER CAPERTON

Born October 16, 1843, in Georgetown, DC. Enlisted as private for the war at Union, Monroe County, VA, August 2, 1862, in Otey's Battery of Virginia Artillery where I served until transferred to the First Maryland Battery in 1865. Remained until the close of the war. Was wounded. Gunshot in the knee on the 9th of April, 1865 at Appomattox Court House the day that Lee surrendered. Was then sent on to Lynchburg where I was paroled some time in April 1865. Never a prisoner of war.

JOHN HENRY CHUNN

Born in St, Mary's County, MD, March 27, 1839. Enlisted as private in Company B, First Maryland Infantry in Richmond August 27, 1862. In which command I served until the close of the war. (Re-enlisted in Second Maryland) Slightly wounded at the battle of Winchester the time we ran Milroy out of there in the summer of 1863. Again slightly wounded at the Battle of Gettysburg. Wounded severely at the Battle of the Weldon Railroad in 1864. Sent from there to the Chimborazo Hospital in Richmond where I was two months before I was convalescent. Then sent back to my command near Petersburg where I remained until captured April 2, 1865, and sent to Point Lookout Prison where I remained till released June 2, 1865. I was in all the battles that my command was engaged in except two that they were in during the time I was laid up with my wound at Chimborazo.

GEORGE WASHINGTON CITY

Born at Washington, DC, September 13, 1835. Enlisted as First Assistant Engineer in Confederate Navy (after having resigned from the same position in the U.S. Navy) July 1, 1861. I was first assigned to duty on the *Patrick Henry* stationed at City Point, VA. After a short time on the *Patrick Henry* was transferred to the gunboat *Richmond* on the Potomac River. Was ordered from here temporally to relive Chief Engineer Ramsey at the Norfolk Naval Yard. After his resumption of duties was ordered to gunboat *Arkansas* at Memphis, TN. Was on the *Arkansas* when she made her fight on the Mississippi River on her way to relive Vicksburg. At Vicksburg was sent to the hospital sick and was still in hospital when the gunboat *Arkansas* was set fire to and blown up by order of Captain Brown at Baton Rouge, LA. A few days before the evacuation was ordered to Jackson, MS, and from there to Savannah, GA. From this point was dispatched to destroy Federal gunboats cruising off Apalachicola, FL. Returned thence to Savannah. Was on a gunboat accompanying the ironclad gunboat *Atlanta* in the attack on Federal Fleet off Ft. Pulaski. On the capture of the *Atlanta* returned to Savannah where I remained till General Sherman captured the city. At the fall of Savannah went to Augusta, GA, on the gunboat *Malcon* where I remained until General Joseph E. Johnston surrendered at North Carolina.

RICHARD CONTEE

Born on Plantation Pleasant Prospect, Prince George County, MD, February 8, 1836. Enlisted as volunteer aide on General Elzey's staff June 1, 1861. My commission as first lieutenant and aide-de-camp on his staff was dated July 21, 1861. Served with General Elzey in this capacity until June 1863 when I resigned and went with my wife to nurse my brother Charles at Winchester, VA. Then, after this, on July 3, 1863, joined General Richard Ewell on the battlefield of Gettysburg as an aide-de-camp and as a volunteer officer. Received a slight flesh wound in the arm in this engagement. Remained in this capacity as a volunteer aide to General Ewell till winter when I went to Richmond and was appointed Major on General G.W. Smith's staff by President Davis. But the war ended before I could join my command. Never captured.

GEORGE GRISWOLD COOMBE

Born January 3, 1839, in Washington, DC. Enlisted at Richmond May 1861 as private in First Maryland Light Artillery, Captain Snowdon Andrews commanding. Remained in aforesaid command until discharged in the winter of 1865 in front of Petersburg, having served out my term of enlistment, which was for three years or the war if shorter. Was in all the battles and skirmishes that my command engaged in during my stay with them. Never wounded and never captured.

CHARLES WORTHINGTON DORSEY

Born in Howard County, MD, and as a member of the Howard County Dragoons, a Maryland Milita company, crossed the Maryland border to Leesburg, VA, with about 75 members of the company. In the first part of June 1861 we did patrol duty without being mustered into service for about two weeks. Then enlisted at Leesburg June 1861 as private in Company G, Seventh Virginia Cavalry. Was promoted to orderly sergeant. Was transferred to Company A, First Maryland Cavalry in July 1862. Was honorably discharged in July, 1864—time of service having expired. Then enlisted as a private in Company D, Forty-third Virginia Cavalry under Colonel Mosby, in which command I remained until paroled in June 1865. Was taken prisoner at South Mountain, Frederick County, MD. After being imprisoned at Fort Delaware for about four months was exchanged. Was in the following battles: Kelley's Ford, Sheets Mills, Kernstown, McDowell, Cedar Creek, Harrisonburg, Cross Keys, Port Republic, and all the battles and skirmishes my commands were engaged in.

WILLIAM DONAHUE

Born at Baltimore City. Enlisted April 1861 in North Carolina as private in Company A, Twenty-seventh North Carolina Infantry. Discharged April 12, 1861, at Goldsboro, North Carolina (War over). In all actions in which my command was engaged vise New Bern, Fort Macon, Wise, Fort Kinston, and others.

GEORGE WASHINGTON DOFFLEMYER

Born in Page County, Virginia. Enlisted April 1861 at Luray, Page County as a private in Company C, Seventh Virginia Cavalry. Was in the battles of First Manassas, Romney, Kernstown, Harrisonburg, and all other battles and skirmishes my command was engaged in. After General Lee surrendered, went home. Was not paroled. Never took the oath.

CHARLES FRANCIS DALLAN

Born in Baltimore August 24, 1834. Enlisted as a private in the Chesapeake Artillery, Fourth Maryland Battery, Captain William D. Brown, in the spring of 1862. Was in all the engagements my battery took part in from the First Battle of Fredericksburg to the close of the war. Acted as Provost Guard at Bowling Green, Caroline County, VA, during the winter of 1862 and 1863. Was slightly wounded at the Second Fredericksburg battle and the battle of Gettysburg, but did not leave my command. Was taken prisoner at Fort Gregg April 2, 1865, and sent to Point Lookout where I remained until June 28, 1865. Shortly before being released acted as Sergeant Major of the pen.

JOHN FREDERICK DITUS

Born in Baltimore January 1, 1843. Enlisted August 4, 1862, at Richmond as a private in Company C, First Maryland Cavalry. The company served as Company L, in the First Virginia Cavalry until after the First Maryland Campaign at which time the First Maryland was made up at Winchester, VA. Was in the following named battles: Second Manassas, Chantilly, Antietam, Trevilian, Pollard's Farm, Williamsport, Second Cold Harbor, the raid to Catlett's Station. Dismounted with Company A, Second Maryland Infantry on raid to Moorefield and Petersburg. Served until the close of the war. Never took the oath and was not paroled.

JOHN HENRY DURKINS

Born in Ireland. My parents moved to Baltimore City yet I was a small child. Where I lived until going South in 1861. Enlisted May 21, 1861, at Point of Rocks as a private in Company B, First Maryland Regiment for one year. Was honorably discharged when my term of service had expired in August 1862. During the same month in 1862 re-enlisted at Richmond in Company K, First Maryland Cavalry, Captain George Gaither. Was wounded in the hand by a musket ball at the First Battle of Manassas, also at Chancellorsville by a saber cut over the head. Was taken prisoner early in 1865 at Brandy Station. Was sent to Baltimore City Jail and released when the war was over. Was in the following named battles: First Manassas, Second Manassas, Chancellorsville, Mason's Hill, Munson's Hill, Culpeper Court House, Gettysburg, Brandy Station and other battles and skirmishes in which my command were engaged.

JOHN COLBERT DAVIS

Born in Hampton, VA. Enlisted April 1861 at Hampton, VA, as a private in Company E, Thirty-second Virginia Regiment of Infantry. Was transferred to the navy and consigned to duty on board the Gunboat *Jamestown*. Was in the battle between the Merrimack and the Monitor. Paroled at Richmond after the war.

JOHN ROBINSON DAVIS

Born at Norfolk, VA, September 15, 1842. Enlisted April 1861 in Company H, First Virginia Infantry. Mustered in service of the state of Virginia same month and year. Was with my company at Blackburn Ford July 18, 1861, and First Manassas July 21, 1861. Was in Winter Quarters at Centerville when taken ill with Typhoid Fever. Sent to hospital at Richmond where after examination was orders back to my regiment to be then examined by regimental surgeon for my discharge which was done. Returned to Richmond still in critical physical condition. After a short time, through the influence of friends, received a situation in Ordnance Bureau. Remained there a short time my health still being poor. A request was made by Colonel Josiah Gorgas, Chief of Ordnance, for a messenger to carry dispatches abroad. The position was tendered to me which I accepted. I was sent to Wilmington, NC, on a special engine. Sailed for Bermuda and reported to Major Norman S. Walker. In the meantime Major Beverly Tucker had arrived in the Islands on the Steamer *Harriet Pinckney* for Liverpool and as the steamer was under orders to take Hon. C. L. Vallandigham of Ohio to Halifax, was instructed to transfer my package to Major Tucker as he would return to England at once. In a few days the CSS *Florida*, Captain J.W. Maffitt arrived at Bermuda. Her paymaster, Junius Lynch, having died at sea, Captain Maffitt asked Major Walker that I be ordered aboard his ship and he would appointment me Acting Assistant Paymaster, all of which was done and after our arrival at Brest, France, both Captain Maffitt and myself were detached and ordered to Paris. Whilst there the CSS *Rappahannock* had succeeded in escaping from Sheerness Dock Yard and I was ordered to go at once to Calais, France and report to Captain W.P.C. Campbell for duty on the *Rappahannock*. "Did so" and was still on the ship when the end came. Was never wounded or a prisoner.

CHARLES ALOYSIOUS DONNELLY

Born at Emmitsburg, Frederick County, MD. Enlisted April 1861 at Charleston, SC, in Company C, Confederate States (Regular) Infantry for the term of the war. Served in Castle Pickney, Charleston, Fort Sumter, James Island, Stone River and taken prisoner at Fisher's Hill, VA, June 1864, Sent to Camp Morton, Indiana. Released in April of 1865.

PATRICK DUGGAN

Born in Ireland. Age 75 years. Enlisted spring of 1861 at Staunton, VA, in Company B, Seventh Virginia Infantry. Same year detailed as Ward Master at the Staunton Military Hospital C.S.A. where I remained until the end of the war.

GEORGE FREEMAN DARDEN

Enlisted as private in Company K, Thirty-first North Carolina Regiment of Infantry in 1862 at Charleston, SC. Discharged from the Confederate Army in 1865 at Fort Delaware. Was at the time a second lieutenant. My occupation is watchmaker and I am 70 tears old.

EDWARD CHRISTIAN DEPPISH

Born July 11, 1831, in Baltimore. Enlisted in Company G, First Maryland Regiment of Infantry as second lieutenant at Harpers Ferry on May 19, 1861. In this command I served until the regiment was disbanded at Charlottesville in the summer of 1862. Re-enlisted October 1863 in First Virginia Cavalry as a private. Served in this command until General Robert E. Lee surrendered at Appomattox Court House. Was captured in the battle of Strasburg October 9, 1864. Was incarcerated in Point Lookout Prison where I remained till the expiration of the war when I was released. Never wounded. Was in all the battles that my command engaged in.

Austin Nelson Dempsey

Born in Baltimore in 1841. Enlisted as a private in the spring of 1862 in Letcher's Battery of Light Artillery a Richmond. In which command I served till the expiration of the war. Was in all the engagements my command participated in. Never Wounded. Was captured a few days before the surrender at Appomattox Court House. Was sent as a prisoner of war to the Old Capitol Prison in Washington, DC, where I remained a prisoner until the surrender, which was only a day and a half.

Thomas Jefferson Devine

Born in New York, NY, December 24, 1833. Enlisted as a private May 1861 at Harpers Ferry in the Thirteenth Virginia Regiment of Infantry for one year. In the evacuation of Manassas Junction in the spring of 1862. Was injured in the leg so badly had to be sent to the hospital in Richmond where I remained until recovered. Then re-enlisted in Nineteenth Virginia regiment of Militia (infantry) doing duty in and around Richmond. In which command I remained till General Robert E. Lee surrendered at Appomattox Court House April 9, 1865. Never captured.

John Dunning

Born in Greensborough, Caroline County, MD, on March 10, 1837. Enlisted in Upperville, VA, in Company D, in Colonel John S. Mosby's command in the spring of 1863. In this command I remained during the balance of the war. Surrendering in the early part of May in Winchester to General Hancock, federal general. Wounded in the left thigh (gunshot flesh wound) in a cavalry fight near Upperville in the summer of 1864. The wound was a slight one not necessitating my going to the hospital. Took a ten day furlough and went to Richmond instead. After which I reported back to my command for duty. Was captured in Snickersville in the summer of 1864, but only remained a prisoner a few minuets when I made my escape. Was paroled when surrendering to General Hancock and returned to Maryland.

Roscoe Etherridge

Born in Enfield, NC. Enlisted February 1863 at Wilmington, NC, in Company K, Tenth North Carolina Artillery. Disbanded April 13, 1865, near Raleigh, NC. Saw service at Fort Davis, Fort Lee, Fort Hill and guarding bridges with my command at all times except when in the hospital.

JOHN THOMAS FERRAL

Born Prince George County, MD. Enlisted at Harpers Ferry in May 1861 in Company D, First Maryland Regiment as a private. Was discharged August 1862. Re-enlisted August 1862 in Company B, Second Maryland Cavalry. Received a wound in the knee by a saber stroke at Gettysburg. Was taken prisoner on Romney Pike and sent to Camp Chase, Ohio. Was transferred from there to Point Lookout from which place I was exchanged after having been a prisoner for about eleven months. Was in the following battles: Winchester, Harrisonburg, Cross Keys, Port Republic, Gain's Mills, Malvern Hill, Gettysburg, Fisher's Hill, Leetown, Bunker Hill, Greenland Gap, Independence, Moorefield. Paroled near Appomattox Court House April 11, 1865.

CHARLES DANIEL FUNK

Born at Baltimore City April 18, 1844. Enlisted June 1862 at Richmond in Company C, Fifth Virginia Cavalry. Served two years in that command. Then transferred to Company D, First Maryland Cavalry on July 30, 1864. Served as a private in both commands. Engaged in all the battles and skirmishes in which both regiments participated in. Wounded in the leg by a fragment of a shell at the battle of Brandy Station. Lost the thumb off my left hand in the Valley of Virginia. Never a prisoner or paroled.

WILLIAM JAMES FAHERTY

Born Washington, DC, July 1, 1841. Enlisted as fourth corporal "Beauregard Rifles at Manassas, VA, May 29, 1861. Company disbanded November 1861. This company for a time was attached as Company F in the First Virginia Infantry. When I re-enlisted was mustered in as first lieutenant in Company F, Twenty-third Virginia Cavalry May 1863 at Buffalo Gap, VA.

In December 1864 was assigned to the Secret Service of the Confederacy under the direct supervision of the then Secretary of War, John C. Breckinridge. Remained on this duty until the termination of the war. Never paroled and never surrendered.

Was for a few months a volunteer in Company A, Seventeenth Virginia Infantry in which organization he was engaged in the battle of Seven Pines May 31 and June 1, 1862. Also fought in First Manassas July 21, 1861, New Market May 18, 1863, Charlestown October 18, 1863. Subsequently in all of the Valley Campaign in June 1864 under General Jubal Early.

JUNIUS WOODSON FOWLKES

Born in Nottaway County, VA, in 1843. Enlisted in the Second Company of Richmond Howitzers at Bethel Church, VA, November 1861. Enlisted for the war. Was in service three and a half years. Never was captured. Was in the battle of Wynn's Mill near Yorktown April 1862; Williamsburg May 5, 1862; Missionary Ridge, Resaca, Kennessaw Mountain, Altoona and the battles around Atlanta as well as some smaller engagements on retreat from Dalton to

Atlanta. Never wounded. Surrendered at Hamburg, SC, under General Joseph E. Johnson about April 20, 1865.

JAMES HENRY FOSTER

Born at King William Court House, VA, September 14, 1838. Enlisted at Richmond May 24, 1861, as a private in Company B, Twenty-first Virginia Regiment of Infantry. Mustered out of this regiment at expiration of service May 24, 1862. Re-enlisted in Company B, Sixth Virginia Battalion of Infantry as a private June 14, 1862. In a few days was elected orderly sergeant of Company B of this command with which I remained till after the fall of Richmond in the spring of 1865 when the Battalion was disbanded. Slightly wounded at the battle of Kernstown March 1862 but remained with the command. Never captured. Surrendered when General Robert E. Lee surrendered at Appomattox Court House April 9, 1865.

CHARLES HOWARD FITZ PATRICK

Born in Baltimore City December 23, 1837. Enlisted as a private in the Baltimore Heavy Artillery June 6, 1861. Then was transferred to Company B, Ninth Virginia Infantry. John D. Merrick was captain of the company. I was elected second lieutenant of this company. Was stationed at Craney Island. Then was detailed to the Norfolk Naval Yard as a skilled machinist. Transferred to Chief of Police, Forty-first Virginia Regiment of Infantry as assistant. At the evacuation of Norfolk transferred to the Provost Marshal's Office, General Winder commanding. Detailed as special officer to General Randolph, Secretary of War. Never wounded and never captured.

RICHARD TILGHMAN GILMOR

Born at "Glen Ellen" Baltimore County, MD, August 14, 1840. Educated at home and in Baltimore City. Held on $13,000 bail for participation in riot of 19 April 1861. Went South late in May 1861 to avoid bench warrant. Was stopped at Fortress Monroe and taken aboard US Sloop of War *Cumberland*. Was released by Pendergast and ordered back to Baltimore. Reached Hampton, VA, same night and walked 35 miles to Grove Wharf on the James River and there took Steamer *Glen Cove* for Richmond. There joined and helped form William H. Murray's company and was mustered in the C.S.A. by Adjutant General Samuel Cooper 18 June 1861. After some few days proceeded to Winchester and was elected second lieutenant Company H, First Maryland Infantry. Late in June 1861 marched with the regiment to First Manassas. In April 1862 marched with regiment from Gordonsville to the Valley. Was in the affair at Front Royal and was Provost Marshal at that place. Then to Winchester and was Provost Marshal there until relieved by the Twenty-seventh Virginia regiment (Stonewall Brigade) and rejoined the First Maryland same night. Was in the battle of Cross Key's June 6 & 8. Mustered out of service June 19, 1862, at Staunton having served one year and one day. Re-enlisted August 1862 in

Company F, Twelfth Virginia Cavalry, Captain Harry Gilmor. Was in several affairs in West Virginia under Brigadier General W. E. Jones. In 1863 assisted in forming Company C, Second Maryland Cavalry and was elected first lieutenant. September same year was in various fights in the Valley and in July 1864 was badly wounded in the leg at Frederick City, MD. Was again wounded in the left side at Opequon Creek in October 1864. After February 4, 1865, was in command of the battalion until disbanded on April 29, 1865. Was paroled by Captain Carr, Pennsylvania Cavalry, at Campbell Court House late in June 1865. The war being over returned to Baltimore City August 9, 1865.

SOLOMON ARTHUR GEPHART

Born at Cumberland, MD. Enlisted in Frederick City, MD, April 20, 1861, as a private in Company A, First Maryland Infantry. Promoted to sergeant, discharged August 1862. Re-enlisted August 1862 in Company A, First Maryland Cavalry with which I remained to close of war. Was in the First Battle of Manassas and other actions in which my commands were engaged.

VINCENT GREEN

Born in Baltimore County, MD. Enlisted August 1861 at Machoda Creek on the Potomac River in the Chesapeake or Fourth Maryland Artillery. Was engaged in Seven Days Battles before Richmond, Fredericksburg, Chancellorsville, Second Manassas, Gettysburg, Warrenton Springs, Mine Run, Weldon Railroad and other actions in which my command took part. Wounded at Fredericksburg in left leg above the knee by a minie ball. Paroled at Appomattox (war over).

HOBSON CHARLES GOODMAN

Born in Cumberland County, VA. Enlisted January 1864 at Atlanta, GA, as a private in Breathed's Battalion. Was wounded in the head by a fragment of a shell at Spotsylvania Court House. Was in the battles of Cedar Creek, Yellow Tavern, Hart's Farm, and other engagements. Was paroled at Danville, VA, June 1865.

SAMUEL THOMAS GLENN

Born in Queen Anne County, MD. Enlisted August 29, 1861, at Eastville, VA, as a private in Company B, Thirty-ninth Virginia Infantry. This company was disbanded on the 9th of February 1862 at which time I received my honorable discharge. Re-enlisted February 10, 1862, at Norfolk, VA, as private in Company C, Sixty-first Virginia Regiment of Infantry. About the 10th of March 1862 I applied for and received a transfer to the Maryland Line and was ordered to report to Head Quarters at Richmond. In obedience to this order I went to Richmond and reported to Major George H. Tyler, with the request to be sent to the First Maryland Regiment. He told me that he could not send me then, but advised me to go to the recruiting office and remain there until opportunity offered to send me to my regiment. Remained in Richmond until June at which time Captain Edward Barn's company was ordered to join the regiment, and I being a member of that company joined it about the 15th of June and so served in my regiment. The regiment was disbanded August 17, 1862, and I was again honorably discharged. Re-enlisted at Richmond August 28, 1862, as a private in Company A. Captain William H. Murray, Second Maryland Infantry, in which company I remained until the surrender of General Lee in April 1865. Was wounded a Gettysburg June 3, 1863, in the lower part of the arm. Was taken prisoner April 2, 1865, near Petersburg. Sent to point Lookout and released from there from that place June 12, 1865. Was engaged in the following battles: First and Second Gaines's Mills, Malvern Hill, Harrison's landing, Second Winchester, Gettysburg, Turkey Ridge, White Oak Swamp, Frazer's Farm, Squirrel Level Road and Hatcher's Run.

Benjamin Gough, M.D.

Born near Leonardtown, Saint Mary's County, MD, December 30, 1835. Enlisted at Sangster's Cross Roads June 1861 as a private in Governor's Mounted Guard, Fourth Virginia Cavalry. Then appointed hospital steward December 1861 and assigned to Inspector General Sorrell's office. Then transferred to Norfolk, then to General Pryor's Third Virginia Infantry, then to Winder Hospital. Paroled at Winder Hospital April 1865.

John Gross

Born at Baltimore. Enlisted June 1861 at Iberville Parish, LA, in Company C, Fifteenth Louisiana as sergeant. Then second lieutenant. Term of service four years. Participated in the following named battles: Meadow Bridge, Mechanicsburg, Gaine's Mills, Malvern Hill, Winchester, Harpers Ferry, Sharpsburg, Gettysburg, and Chancellorsville. Paroled 6 June 1865 at Natchitoches, LA. Wounded in side by minie ball at Chancellorsville.

Mathew Green

Born at Baltimore City March 26, 1835. Enlisted May 1861 at Harpers Ferry in Company D, First Maryland Regiment Infantry for one year. Re-enlisted 1863 in Colonel Mosby's command at Headquarters, Fauquair County, VA, for the war. Was in every battle my regiment was engaged in up to the Battle of Port Republic. Was sent to the Hospital at Charlottesville. Afterwards was discharged at Charlottesville. Paroled at Winchester with Mosby's command after General Lee surrendered.

John Henry Gordon

Born in Anne Arundel County, MD, November 23, 1839. Enlisted at Harpers Ferry in May 1861 in Company G, First Maryland Regiment for four years. Where I remained until mustered out late in the summer of 1862. (Not stated that he re-enlisted in Company B, 35th Virginia Cavalry) Was captured in the battle of Brandy Station on the 9th of June 1863. Was sent to the Old Capitol Prison in Washington, DC, where I remained for two or three weeks when I was exchanged and joined my command in Virginia near the Potomac River. Was in all the engagements that my two commands participated in. My first engagement being the famous Battle of Bull Run Races at Manassas, VA. Went through the West Virginia raid under General Jones. Served through the whole entire war and mustered out in 1865.

ISAREL GRAHAM

Born in Loudon County, VA, May 29, 1833. Enlisted in Winchester as private in Company G, Seventh Virginia Cavalry May 1, 1862. Was transferred from this command to Company A, First Maryland Cavalry May 1, 1864, in which command I served till close of the war. I was in all the battles and engagements that both my commands were in. Never wounded. Captured about the latter part of May 1864 at Pollards Farm. Imprisoned at Elmira, NY. Released from prison at Elmira June 16, 1865—when the war was over and I returned to my home.

ALEXANDER GARDEN

Born at Wyliesburg, Charlotte County, VA, June 25, 1833. Enlisted as a private at Wyliesburg in Company G, Fifty-sixth Virginia Regiment of Infantry on July 1, 1861. Remained in this same command until the end of the war. Was only engaged in one battle during four years and that was the battle of Fort Donelson, TN, which lasted all day and night. General Floyd with his command cut his way out and thus escaped. The rest of the Confederates were captured. Never captured. Never wounded.

WILLIAM OLIVER GREEN

Born in Cecil County, MD, in 1837. Enlisted as a private in Company D, First Maryland Cavalry. In which command remained during the war. Never wounded. Captured near Richmond March 1864 in a fight with General Kilpatrick's Federal command who were trying to take Richmond. Was carried to Point Lookout Federal prison in Maryland. And there remained 12 months when I was released and sent across the lines to Camp Lee to there wait to be exchanged. Was on a furlough in North Carolina when General Robert E. Lee surrendered at Appomattox Court House April, 1865.

FRANCIS THOMAS GROVE

Born January 16, 1845, at Sharpsburg, MD. Enlisted as a private in Company B, Second Virginia Infantry for 12 months. At the expiration of that time re-enlisted in Company F, First Virginia Cavalry (for the war) and remained in this command till close of the war. Was captured at Strasburg, VA, the time General Phil Sheridan made his raid down the Valley. Received gunshot flesh wound in right leg and was left lying on the battlefield of Strasburg all night. This is how I came to be captured. The Yankees picked me up the following morning and sent me to West Building Hospital in Baltimore where I remained a prisoner for sixty days and then exchanged and went back and joined my command and remained with them until General Robert E. Lee surrendered at Appomattox Court House April 9, 1865. First enlisted at Harpers Ferry at the time the Army was being formed and organized in the spring of 1861.

THOMAS HUNTER

Born at Long Green, Baltimore County, MD, August 26, 1837. Enlisted August 25, 1862, at Charlottesville, VA, in Company A, First Maryland Cavalry. Transferred to Second Virginia Cavalry, Col. Thomas Munford. Remained with the latter regiment until after the battle of Sharpsburg. Commissary Sergeant. Taken prisoner at Moorefield, WV, on the retreat from Chambersburg, PA. Just before daylight on a Sunday morning, marched 2 miles then placed in a hollow square until day light that following Monday, then marched about 45 miles to New Creek without any food or water. Thence to Camp Chase, OH. Paroled not to take up arms until exchanged. Taken to camp Lee in Richmond and furloughed for 30 days unless sooner exchanged. Then sent to Lynchburg where I remained until after the surrender of General Lee. Was in all of the engagements of our command with General W. E. Jones in his raid through West Virginia and his destruction of Oil Town, WV, where large quantities of oil were stored.

WILLIAM JAMES CANADY HOLLAND

Born in Worcester County, MD. Enlisted at Culpepper Court House, VA, in February 1862 in Company K, First Virginia Cavalry. Transferred to Company K, First Maryland Cavalry. Was in the following named battles: Seven Pines, Second Manassas, Thoroughfare Gap, Manassas Junction, Trevillian Station, and all others in which my command was engaged. Received a wound in the leg from a minie ball at the Second Battle of Manassas. Was also wounded by a fragment of a shell at Hanover Court House. Was taken prisoner at the Second Battle of Manassas and exchanged. Was paroled at Harpers Ferry, VA.

JOHN HIPKINS

Born in Norfolk, VA. In 1861 I was Master's Mate on board the USS *Vincent* when learning of the secession of Virginia. We were stationed in the Gulf of Mexico. I then tended my resignation stating that it was impossible for me to fight against my own people and principles, respectfully requesting to be sent home in the first passing vessel. In about an hour after I had sent in my resignation I was ordered to consider myself under arrest and confined to my quarters. Spoken to by none and scowled at by all, on the fourth or fifth day of my confinement the transport *Rhode Island* came to anchor near us and I was sent on board and stowed away below. A hammock was assigned me. After a voyage of nine days we arrived in New York harbor. I was then taken to Fort Lafayette where I remained twenty months. I then enlisted in November 1863 at Richmond as a private in Company F, Forty-third Virginia Cavalry. Our company was disbanded on April 17, 1865. Was in the following named battles: Paris, Middleburg, Aldie, Falls Church, Fairfax Station, Upperville, Salem, and the battles and skirmishes my command was engaged in after my enlistment. Was wounded in the leg by a pistol ball at Falls Church.

SAMUEL SYLVESTER HUDSON

Born in Washington, DC. Enlisted May 1861 at Sheperdstown, VA, as a private in Company B, Second Virginia Infantry. Was taken prisoner in 1862 at Kernstown and sent to Fort Delaware where I remained for five or six months before being exchanged. Was in the following named battles: Kernstown, Chancellorsville, Fredericksburg, and Gettysburg. Was again taken prisoner at Sheperdstown and sent to Camp Chase from which place I was paroled in April 1865.

WILLIAM HANDY HOBBS

Born in Baltimore City. Enlisted March 18, 1861, at Charleston, SC, as a private in Company C, Lucas' Battery of Regular Artillery. Was made drummer for about six months. Was transferred to Company E, Harry Gilmor's cavalry March 1864. Was wounded at Fort Wagner. Was taken prisoner at New Hope, VA, and sent to Camp Morton, Indiana, and released May 22, 1865. Besides the battles of Fort Wagner and New Hope, was in many other battles and skirmishes that my commands were engaged.

JOHN STEPHEN HALBIG

Born in Baltimore City. Enlisted for one year, July 1861 at Aquia Creek, VA, as a private in Company H, Forty-seventh Virginia Infantry. Was honorably discharged when my time of service had expired. Re-enlisted July 1862 at Richmond as a private in Company E, Second Maryland Infantry. Was promoted to corporal. Was wounded in the right shoulder by a minie ball at Seven Pines May 31, 1862. Was wounded in the right leg by a minie ball at the battle of Winchester (with Milroy). Also wounded at Gettysburg by five musket balls in my right arm July 3, 1863. Was taken prisoner and sent to the West Buildings Hospital in Baltimore. Thence to Fortress Monroe from which place I was exchanged in September 1863. Was again taken prisoner at the fall of Richmond and sent to Camp Lee where I remained until paroled July 4, 1865. Was in the following named battles: Yorktown, Williamsburg, Seven Pines, Strasburg, Winchester, Aquia Creek, and other battles and skirmishes my commands were engaged in.

ENOCH GEORGE HEDGES

Born in Berkley County, VA, April 8, 1817. Enlisted May 1861 at Winchester as a private in Company F, Seventh Virginia Cavalry for the war.

Captured near Martinsburg. Sent to Cumberland, MD, and there exchanged. At the time was Commissary Sergeant. In battles of Winchester, Gettysburg and all other actions my command was engaged.

JOHN DAVID HANSON

Born in Charles County, MD. Enlisted July 11, 1861, at Richmond in Company I, First Maryland Regiment for one year. Re-enlisted in Company B, Twenty-fifth Virginia Battalion July 1862 for the war. Rank was first sergeant. Captured at Amelia Springs April 6, 1865. Sent as a prisoner to Point Lookout. Remained there until June 13, 1865, then paroled (war ended). In the battles of Front Royal, Winchester, Munson's Hill, and all other actions my commands were engaged. Also acted as one of the Provost guards at Richmond for six months in 1862.

WILLIAM EDWARD HEAD

Born November 5, 1836, in Iridell County, NC. Enlisted as a private in 1861 at Jonesborough, TN, in Company A, Sixtieth Tennessee Regiment of Infantry in which command I remained till end of the war. Received gunshot wound in left hand at Vicksburg July 3, 1863. Participated in all the battles that my command was engaged in. never captured. Was sick in Hospital at Macon, GA, when General Wilson entered the town and took position of it. I surrendered to him in 1865.

ANDREW JACKSON HOPKINS

Born in Kent County, VA, on the 22nd of April 1832. Enlisted at Richmond on April 16, 1861, as a corporal in Company H, Fifteenth Regiment of Infantry in which command I served during the entire war. Was engaged in all the battles and skirmishes that my regiment engaged in. Was captured in a skirmish in Buckingham County, VA, by Sheridan's Cavalry the night before General Robert E, Lee surrendered. I was only held prisoner for two days when I was paroled and permitted to return to my home—the war being over. Wounded in the right leg at Battle of Malvern Hill. Gunshot flesh wound. Never left the regiment.

ROBERT FIELDING HITCHCOCK

Born in Richmond, VA, August 1847. Enlisted in Richmond as a private March 1861 in Company B, First Virginia Regiment of Infantry for one year. Was discharged before the expiration of that time on account of my youth and sickness. (By wish or desire of my guardian Mr. Haxall) Then went to school until 1862 when I volunteered to work in the Confederate Arsenal in Richmond until August 1863 when I enlisted in Company D, Col. Harry Gilmor's Cavalry command in which I remained till the end of the war. Was captured at the evacuation of Richmond by General Robert E. Lee and was carried to the old Libby Prison in Richmond where I remained two or three weeks when General Lee surrendered at Appomattox Court House when I was paroled to go to my home. Never wounded.

GEORGE WILLIAM HOFFMAN

Born in Baltimore August 1841. Enlisted as a private in Company F, First Maryland Infantry sometime in April 1861 at Harpers Ferry. Served in this command some 15 months till after the Seven Days fighting around Richmond when the regiment was honorably discharged by order of the Secretary of War. Received slight flesh wound at Port Republic and Cross Keys, but not sufficiently bad as to cause me to be sent to a hospital. Remained all the time with my regiment. Was captured at Frederick, MD, during the summer of 1862 the day after the battle of Sharpsburg or Antietam. Remained a prisoner until the end of the war.

THOMAS SOMERVILLE JOHNSON

Born near Prince Frederick, Calvert County, MD, in 1843. Enlisted in the Baltimore Light Artillery C.S.A. at Frederick City in September 1862. Was wounded by a shell at Hazel River, Culpepper, VA, September 1863. After return from hospital served with the company until close of the war. Surrendered and paroled at Lynchburg, VA, 1865. Participated in the following named regular engagements and numerous skirmishes: Harpers Ferry, Sharpsburg, Kernstown, Winchester, Gettysburg, Culpeper, Woodstock, Martinsburg, Moorefield, Waynesboro and Maurytown.

EDWIN JAMES

Born at Washington, DC. Enlisted in Company H, First Virginia Regiment C.S.A. in the latter the later part of 1861 at Richmond for the term of one year. Re-enlisted for the war in 1862. Transferred to Company A, Maryland Line, Col. Bradley T. Johnson and served to close of war. Participated in the following battles: First Manassas (slightly wounded), Seven Pines, Gaines' Mills. Surrendered at Appomattox Court House. War over.

THOMAS ANDERSON JEFFERS

Born Edgefield, SC. Enlisted at Charleston, SC, April 1861 as a private in the Beaufort District Troops, Hampton's Legion. Elected second lieutenant Company B, Second South Carolina Cavalry July 1862. Disbanded at Greensboro N.C. April 1865 (War over). In battles of Fredericksburg, Brandy Station, Seven Pines, Seven Days before Richmond, Second Manassas, Sharpsburg, Fort Fisher, Gettysburg, and others in which my command was engaged.

BENJAMIN RURK JENNINGS

Born in Baltimore City in 1840. On the 21st day of May 1861 I left Baltimore, taking a train at Camden Station for Harpers Ferry where on or about the 24th of the same month I enlisted as a private in Company A, First Maryland Regiment of Infantry. From Harpers Ferry in June and Winchester in July, I participated in all of the movements of my command with the exception of the battle of Manassas up to the time of going into Winter Quarters near Centerville. From Winter Quarters in March 1862 was with the Regiment and took part in all of its marches and actions in the Valley Campaign up to Winchester. Took to the vicinity of Richmond in June where our regiment took part in the engagement of Gaines' Mills or First Battle of Cold Harbor. In July 1862 I was sick in Richmond. Was told to go to Captain James R. Hubert, being at the house of Mrs. Parr, whose family physician attended me. I rejoined my command at Gordonsville the later part of July. When on the 17th day of August the First Maryland Infantry was disbanded and on the next I received my discharge at Charlottesville. On the 19th I started for Lynchburg to see a brother in the hospital there. He had been wounded in the head, but I was too late to see him. He had died from the effects of his wound. I then went to Alabama near the city of Montgomery, where my father had retired from Norfolk and Richmond (Railroad). Ill health compelling him to decline the position of Hospital Surgeon. Here I found another brother dying from sickness contracted in the Army of Virginia. After my brother's death, my fathers affairs, and the state of his health were such that I determined to remain with him and the other members of the family for the present.

In the latter part of May 1864 I enlisted in Company A, Second Maryland Infantry. On the 5th of June I joined my company and from that time I was with my command in all of its movements and actions from White Oak Swamp, Turkey Ridge or Bend, the trenches at Petersburg. The two battles on the Weldon Railroad, Frazier's Farm, and Squirrel Level Road. The movements to the right of the line and into Winter Quarters in November. In the later part of December 1864 we went on the Smithfield trip and a terrible experience we had. Suffering greatly from the bitter cold and sleety weather. On the 5th of February 1865 was in the battle of Hatcher's Run where I was wounded in the leg by a minnie ball. Was sent to the Robinson Hospital in Richmond. Then to the Chimborazo Hospital and then to private quarters. Was in Richmond at the time that city was evacuated. Witnessed the firing and burning of the Training Ship *Patrick Henry*. The blowing up of a Confederate gunboat. The entering of the first Union Troops in the city. The arrival of President Lincoln on his visit to Richmond and his departure the next day on his return trip to Washington. Sometime after General Lee had surrendered I was with about 150 other prisoners marched from the Jackson Hospital to the Libby Prison where we were confined two days and three nights. Then we were sent to Newport News and liberated on the 3rd of July 1865.

CHARLES T. JONES
Born 15 miles from Cincinnati, OH, March 12, 1819. Enlisted in Richmond on the passage of the act of secession for the defense of Richmond in Captain

Bowling Baker's company, Colonel A. Mcannovy's regiment, General G.W.C. Lee's brigade. Never was wounded or a prisoner. Was paroled in Danville, VA, after the surrender of General Lee.

JOHN J. JOHNSON

Enlisted as a private at Harpers Ferry May 8, 1861, in Company E, First Maryland Infantry. In which command I remained till the summer of 1862 when it was disbanded by order of the Secretary of War. Then enlisted as a Confederate sailor where I remained until the surrender of the Naval Brigade in 1865.

WILLIAM ALFRED JARBOE

Born in Prince George's County, MD, March 4, 1844. At the age of eighteen I left my father's house in August 1862 and ran the blockade across the Potomac River from Pope's Creek in Charles County into Westmorland County, VA. From there proceeded to Richmond where I arrived the third day after leaving home. In Richmond I met many of my father's friends from Maryland. Among them our family physician Dr. James Boyle, who persuaded me not to enlist on account of my headache which had been very delicate from my infancy, but to remain in Richmond until I should get older and probably strong enough to go into military service, promising to procure a civil position for me. Hence, after being in the city for some months, Major C. D. Hill, Government Quartermaster gave me a clerkship in his department which position I held for several months until I received an appointment as accountant in the office of the Second Auditor of the Treasury. I remained there until the first of the year 1864. Then resigned the position and joined Mosby's Cavalry. But soon after my enlistment was unfortunately captured together with two others of the same command while asleep in the lines of Loudoun County, VA. Was imprisoned five months in the Old Capitol Prison in Washington, DC, and nine months in Fort Warren, Boston Harbor from which place I was released after the close of the war. Was shot at after I had surrendered by a Yankee soldier not more than three feet from me and after a seemingly miraculous escape would have been murdered by my captors had it not been for the prompt arrival of the major of their command. Was again shot at by a sentry for looking out of a window while a prisoner in the Old Capitol and again escaped by a hair's breadth.

JOHN HANSON KEPLER

Born Washington, DC, August 2, 1838. Mustered in the service as corporal in Company D, First Virginia at Richmond, April 21, 1861. Served through the war as corporal, 2nd sergeant, and 1st sergeant of said company. Said regiment Kemper's Brigade, Pickett's Division, Longstreet's Corps, A.N.V. Slightly wounded at Frazier's Farm, taken prisoner at Gettysburg in the charge of Pickett's Division. Sent to Point Lookout. Remaining at the latter place about ten months, then exchanged with a boatload of sick. Captured a second time at

Five Forks. Sent to Point Lookout. Paroled first part of June 1865 and sent to Richmond.

Engaged in the following battles: Bull Run, Manassas, Williamsburg, Sharpsburg, Fredericksburg, Suffolk, Gettysburg, Dinwiddie Court House, Five Forks, and others of less note.

EDWARD SCHOOLFIELD KING

Born in Baltimore City. Enlisted May1861 at Harpers Ferry as a private in Company D, First Maryland Infantry. Promoted sergeant. Discharged August 1862 term of service expired. Re-enlisted September 1862 in Breathed's Artillery. Wounded in leg on return from Gettysburg by a musket ball. Captured July 11, 1863, at Hagerstown, MD. Sent to Baltimore City Jail, then to Point Lookout. Prisoner until May 1865. In all the battles and actions in which my commands were engaged.

JOHN THOMAS KEATS, M.D.

Born in Queen Anne County, MD. Enlisted May 1863 at Richmond. Was a private in Company B, First Maryland Cavalry. Detailed to Assistant Surgeon September 1863. Taken prisoner May 8, 1864 in Talbot County, MD, whilst on furlough. Released May 9, 1865, from Fort McHenry. In all the actions in which my command was in.

DANIEL MURRAY KEY

Born in Anne Arundel County, MD, in 1841. Enlisted June 1861 at Harpers Ferry as a private in Company D, First Maryland Regiment Infantry. Time of service having expired, was honorably discharged late in the summer of 1862. Re-enlisted in the fall in the Thirty-fifth Virginia, White's Battalion, Rosser's Brigade of Cavalry. In which command I remained until the end of the war. Was wounded in the knee by a musket ball in the battle of Parker's Store on Sunday, November 19, 1863. Producing a stiff knee, which incapacitated me for active duty for the balance of the war. Was taken prisoner at the battle of Brandy Station. Imprisoned in the Old Capitol Building (Prison) at Washington, DC, for about two weeks, when I was exchanged. Was in the hospital at Charlottesville at the time of General Lee's surrender.

CHARLES AUGUSTUS KRANS

Born in Baltimore City. Enlisted May 1861 at Richmond as a private in Company A, Seventh Virginia Cavalry. Was wounded in the battle of Cross Keys in the right wrist by a fragment of shell. Was transferred to the First Maryland Cavalry at Richmond in June 1863. Was wounded in the left wrist by a musket ball on the Valley Pike near Middletown. Was in the hospital from this wound for nearly one year. After this I was not able to do the regular army duties and was detailed as quartermaster sergeant. Was taken prisoner at Front Royal. Sent to Fort McHenry. After five days confinement there was exchanged.

On the eve of my exchange a fellow prisoner in the officer's quarters wanted a volunteer to carry a letter to President Davis. No one offering, I did. Took the letter and sewed it up in the lining of my pants and delivered in person to President Davis. This officer was sentenced to be shot as a spy, but was not for I have seen him lately. Was in the following battles: Raid in West Virginia, Greenland Gap, Oakland, Oil Wells (Town), Moorefield, and many skirmishes.

JOHN FRANCIS KEY

Born in Annapolis, MD, Enlisted June 1, 1861, at Harpers Ferry as a private in Company D, First Maryland Infantry. Enlisted for one year. Was honorably discharged., time of service having expired in August 1862. Re-enlisted in Breathed's Battery the same year. Was wounded in the right arm by a musket ball at the battle of Cross Keys. Was taken prisoner at Culpeper County, VA, in 1863. Sent to the Old Capitol Prison and from there to Point Lookout. Was in the following named battles: First Manassas, Mason's Hill, Munson's Hill, Rappahannock Station, Harrisonburg, Cross Keys, Union, Opequon, Gettysburg, Chancellorsville, and all other battles and engagements my command took part in.

FRANCIS PATRICK KELLY

Born in County Tyrone, Ireland. Enlisted in 1861 at Petersburg, VA, in Company B, Twelfth Virginia Infantry. Transferred to Branch's Battery 1862. In 3 engagements at Five Forks. The piece of artillery I was attached to was covered up at the explosion of the crater. We were in the trenches around Petersburg a long time. Captured at Petersburg April 4, 1865. Paroled April 10, 1865. Was also a prisoner at Point Lookout. Never wounded.

WILLIAM FRANCIS KNOX

Born in Baltimore City. Entered the Service of the Confederacy in June 1862 under Secretary of War Randolph (Secret Service) where I remained until May 1864. Then enlisted May 1864 at Yellow Tavern as a private in Baltimore Light Artillery for the war. Acted as quartermaster sergeant of the battery. Was in all the actions in which the battery was engaged. Paroled at Lynchburg after General Lee's surrender April 1865.

JAMES LUSBY

Born in Baltimore City. Enlisted May 1861 at Harpers Ferry in Company F, First Maryland Infantry. Discharged August 1862 at Richmond. Re-enlisted February 1863 for the war in Breathed's Artillery. Transferred to Company F, First Maryland Cavalry August 1864. Paroled at Appomattox April 9, 1865. Battles engaged in: First Manassas, Winchester, Front Royal, Port Republic, Harrisonburg, Cross Keys, Rappahannock Bridge, Wilderness, Seven Pines, Chancellorsville, Sharpsburg, Gettysburg and other actions.

JAMES LAMATES

Born in Baltimore. Enlisted May 1861 at Point of Rocks, Frederick County, MD, as a private in Company B, First Maryland Regiment (Infantry). Discharged August 1862, term of enlistment has expired. In the latter part of August 1862 re-enlisted in Company E, Second Maryland Infantry. Wounded at Gettysburg in the left shoulder by a musket ball at Culp's Hill. Captured at Gettysburg. Sent as a prisoner to Davis's Island, NY. Exchanged in September 1863. Again captured at battle of Weldon Railroad August 1864. Taken to Point Lookout. Released April 1865. In all Actions which my command was engaged.

WILLIAM HENRY LUCAS

Born in Baltimore City. Enlisted April 1861 at Columbia, SC, in Company C, First South Carolina Infantry. Remained with my command until the close of the war. Was in the battles of Ox Hill, Mine Run, Ream's Station, Wilderness, Sharpsburg, and all the actions my command was engaged in. Was paroled at Dallas, NC. Received a wound in the right arm by a musket ball at Gaines' Mills. Was also severely wounded in the head at Columbia, SC, being struck by one of the Twenty-fifth Ohio Infantry with the butt of an axe.

THOMAS GEORGE LECHLINDER

Born in Frederick County, MD. Enlisted May 1, 1861, at Point of Rocks as a private in Company A, First Maryland Regiment Infantry. Was wounded in the arm at Bristoe Station in 1862. Time of service having expired, re-enlisted June 1862 for the war. Was in the following named battles: Bull Run, Fredericksburg, Winchester, Frederick City, Antietam and other battles and skirmishes my command engaged in.

DRURY LACY LUNSDON

Born Raleigh, NC. Enlisted March 18, 1861, at Columbia, SC, as a private in Company H, Second South Carolina Cavalry. Was wounded in left side June 1863 by three shots from an Army pistol at Brandy Station. Was in all the battles and skirmishes my command was engaged in. Surrendered with General Joseph E. Johnson at Goldsboro, NC.

GERORGE LEMMON

Born in Baltimore August 25, 1835. Enlisted as a private at Richmond in Company H, First Maryland Infantry July 1861. Appointed Captain to raise a company September 1861. Sent to Charleston, SC, to bring Maryland men from Fort Sumter in February 1862. Was appointed Volunteer Aide on General Hood's staff May 1862. On General Archer's staff June 1862. Appointed first lieutenant of Artillery and Ordinance Officer August 1862. Assigned to General Archer's Brigade. Was captured near Cashtown, PA, July 5, 1863. Returned to Richmond September 1864. Exchanged December 1864. Was then placed on duty at the Arsenal in Richmond January and February 1865. Assigned to

General Payne as Ordnance Officer March 1865. Transferred to General Munford April 1865. Ordered to General Joseph E. Johnson's Army April 9, 1865. Reported to him at Greensboro, but assigned to no duty. Left there the day before the surrender and returned to Baltimore July 1865. Was in the battle of Manassas as a private, Seven Pines as Aide to General Hood, around Richmond as A.A.A.G. to General Archer. Also in the battles of Slaughter Mountain, Chantilly, Harpers Ferry, Shepherdstown, Fredericksburg and Chancellorsville. Never wounded.

ROMANUS PHILIP LUDWIG

Born in Shenandoah County, VA, December 2, 1846. Enlisted as a private in Company D, Thirty-fifth Virginia (White's) Battalion of Cavalry in which command I remained till the close of the war when General Robert E. Lee surrendered at Appomattox Court House April 9, 1865. Had a horse killed under me and slight flesh wound at the battle of Fisher's Hill October 8, 1864. Was in all the fights that my command—Rosser's Laurel Brigade—was engaged in. Enlisted at Woodstock, VA, April 5, 1863.

THOMAS LUNFORD LOMAX

Born in Fredericksburg, VA, October 11, 1836. Enlisted as a private at King William Court House, VA, in Company K, Thirtieth Virginia Infantry May 22, 1861. Remained in this same command till honorably discharged August 30, 1863, when I was appointed to a clerkship in the War department in Richmond where I remained until the close of the war. Received a severe gunshot wound in the thigh (fracturing the bone badly) at the battle of Sharpsburg September 17, 1862. Here I was captured by the Federal forces and carried to Frederick, MD, and placed in a Federal hospital where I remained until permitted to go to a friend's, Judge Marshall's, house in the city and there kindly cared for and nursed till convalesced (having lain nine months in bed). As soon as strong enough was sent as a prisoner of war to Fort Norfolk, near Norfolk, VA, June 1863. Remained here two months when I was exchanged and sent across the lines incapacitated for active field service on account of the effects of the wound received at Sharpsburg, MD.

JOHN HALLAWAY LYNN

Born July 25, 1841, in Hampshire County, VA. Enlisted in the summer of 1861 in Hardy County, VA, as a private in Captain Hanson McNeal's Independent Company of Cavalry in which command served during the entire war. Received slight flesh wound in the arm. Captured twice. Last time in 1865 an imprisoned (in close confinement) at Fort McHenry where I remained till the expiration of the war. Captured at the same time that Colonel Gilmor of the Second Maryland Cavalry was.

CHARLES MYERS

Born in Austria. Enlisted July 1861 at Nashville as a private in Company F, First South Carolina Heavy Artillery. Served most of my time in Fort Sumter during the bombardment. Captured at Bentonville, NC. Taken to Hart's Island, NY, as a prisoner of war. Released June 17, 1865.

JOHN MARNEY

Born at Manchester, England. Enlisted May 22, 1861, at Harpers Ferry in Company A, First Maryland Infantry as First Sergeant. Term expired August 1862 and discharged at Gordonville. Re-enlisted August 1862 at Richmond in Company A, Second Maryland Infantry. Wounded at Gettysburg on Culp's Hill. A minie ball in the head and a shell fragment in the leg. Captured there and taken to David's Island, NY, September 1863. Paroled and sent to City Point. Discharged from battalion October 1864 at Petersburg on account of the wound received in the Battle of Gettysburg. Battles: First Manassas, Winchester, Gettysburg, and other actions with my command. Was a citizen of Maryland in 1861.

STEPHEN McDONALD

Born in County Monoghan, Ireland. Enlisted March 17, 1862, at Richmond in Company A, Tenth Battalion Heavy Artillery. Left the service after the surrender of General Lee. Was at Appomattox, but did not remain to be paroled. Wounded in the Seven Days Battles in front of Richmond in the elbow by a minie ball. In a number of other actions with the command. Ran the blockade in early part of March 1862. Captured as a spy and delivered to C. S. authorities (before enlistment). I was a citizen of Baltimore for years previous to 1861.

DANIEL McCAULEY

Born in County Limerick, Ireland. Was a citizen of Baltimore in 1861. Enlisted May 1861 at Keysville, VA, as a private in Staurton Hill Battery. Slightly wounded at Fort Fisher in the head by a minie ball. In battles of Wilmington, Newport Barracks, Moorehead City, Roanoke, and others. Taken prisoner near Fort Fisher. Carried to old prison in Wilmington, NC, thence to Fortress Monroe. The war being over was paroled and released in May of 1865.

JOHN IGNATIUS McWILLIAMS

Born at Baltimore January 10, 1836. Enlisted in Co. G, Thirteenth Virginia Infantry as a private on May 24, 1861, at Harpers Ferry. Promoted to sergeant major of the regiment at First Battle of Manassas by Colonel A. P. Hill. The term of service of the company having expired, we were mustered out on May 28, 1862. Remained with the regiment as a volunteer until the latter part of September 1862. On or about the 10th of October 1862 reported to General John H. Winder at Richmond and assigned by him to the Secret Service. Was under his orders until February 1863 when he sent me with sealed orders to report to General Whiting at Wilmington, NC. Was under the latter general until May 1863, then ordered to Richmond. Was elected second lieutenant in Company G, Nineteenth Virginia State Troops and commanded by Governor Letcher. The regiment was stationed in breastworks in front of Richmond and occasionally did guard duty at various prisons in Richmond. I proceeded to the Valley on or about the first of September 1864 for the purpose of joining my old regiment (13th VA). At the battle of Winchester was made a prisoner with others on the 17th of September 1864. Taken to Point Lookout. Remained there until the latter part of March 1865. Then paroled and sent to Richmond (war over two weeks after). Participated in First and Second Manassas, First and Second Winchester, Sharpsburg, and Cross Keys, also skirmishes of Mason and Munson's Hills.

Left Baltimore City on or about May 8, 1861, with 30 young men to proceed to Richmond. Went through Washington City. Put up at James Jackson's "Marshall House" Alexandria, VA. I was delayed here five days in procuring transportation when I proceeded to Richmond with my men and put them in the Columbian Hotel. I returned to Baltimore for more men. Upon my arrival in Baltimore I found it too hot for me. I left with five men for Harpers Ferry. At the latter place I met for the first time Colonel T. J. Jackson (Stonewall). After a short interview he gave me a pass and transportation to Richmond for the purpose of bringing my men to Harpers Ferry. Then being joined by some 30 other young men from Baltimore joined Company G, Thirteenth Virginia Infantry, Colonel A. P. Hill. In May 1865 I returned to Baltimore and on my arrival was arrested and taken before Colonel W. H. Wiegal, Acting Provost Marshal. Taken to Negro Jail and that worthy gave me 12 hours to leave the city, charging me with being in the U.S. employment and recruiting a company for the South. I then went south, returning again in the early part of 1867.

JAMES JACKSON MITCHELL

Born in Kings and Queens County, VA, June 16, 1845. Enlisted March 15, 1862, at Richmond as a private in the President's Guard for the war. This company under the subsequent command of Captain Lucian L. Bass, was incorporated into the Twenty-fifth Battalion of Virginia Infantry, Colonel Wyatt M. Elliott as Company G. Took part in all the actions of this command up to the latter part of 1864 when we were transferred by order of Secretary Seddon to cooperate with Colonel John S. Mosby. Retired at the close of the war.

JOHN D. MAHONY

Born in Ireland. Enlisted May 10, 1861, at Charlestown, SC, as a private in Company G, First South Carolina Artillery. Was wounded at Fort Sumter April 2, 1863, in the breast by a fragment of a shell. Was taken prisoner at Columbia, SC, at the time of Sherman's raid, and sent to Point Lookout. I remained there until Paroled June 15, 1865. Was in the following named battles: Morris Island, James Island, Fort Moultrie, the siege of Sumter, Orangeburg, the capture of the

Yankee supply boat in Stone River and all of the engagements of my command up to the time of my being taken prisoner.

HENRY HAW MATTHEWS

Born at Georgetown, DC, March 24, 1845. Enlisted May 12, 1861, at Alexandria, VA, in the Beauregard Rifles, Captain Frank Schaeffer of Washington, DC, commanding. At the evacuation of Alexandria, May 24, 1861, went with my company to Manassas and reported to General P.G.T. Beauregard for assignment. We were ordered to the Stone Bridge on Bull Run and remained at that point until after the First Manassas affair in which we participated. On July 28, 1861, we were ordered to report to Major Fred Skinner, commanding the First Virginia Infantry at Fairfax Court House. On reporting we took the place of Company F which had been ordered to Norfolk. We remained with the regiment until November of the same year when we organized Stuart's Horse Artillery, Captain John Pelham commanding. I remained with the battery until August 12, 1864. At that time we were in front of Petersburg and near Ream's Station on the Petersburg and Weldon Railroad. I took advantage of the Act of Congress allowing Marylanders to join their own state organizations and was transferred to Company D, First Maryland Cavalry, Captain Warner Welsh commanding. Reported to said company two week later at Woodstock in the Valley of Virginia. I was in all the general engagements in which the Army of Northern Virginia participated and in a great number of smaller affairs in which my commands were engaged. I was wounded at Union, Loudoun County, VA, by a fragment of a shell. Paroled at Richmond June 18, 1865. Quartermaster at the Maryland Line Confederate Soldiers' Home since June 1898.

JAMES LOUIS MAGUIRE

Born at Baltimore July 20, 1832. Left the Naval Yard in Washington, DC, April 17, 1861. Was in the Baltimore riot on the 19th of April 1861. Left Baltimore for Richmond and arrived at the latter city May 20. Following employment in the Richmond Armory until November 1861, was sworn into Confederate Service November 1861 by Captain Sydney G. Lee. Belonged to a local command called the Franklin Buchanan Guard until the evacuation of Norfolk. Was detailed with others by Captain Lee to destroy the Navy Yard, which was successfully done. Joined the First Maryland Infantry Company E at Staunton, Lieutenant John G. Lutts commanding. Participated in all the battles in front of Richmond. Was with the regiment until disbanded at Gordonsville. Then was detailed for service at the Naval Iron Works at Columbus, GA, until 1864. Belonged to a local command in the latter named city. Was detailed by the Quartermaster at Motgomery, AL, to build a leather splitting machine for that department. It was the first of its kind built in the South. Remained in the employment of that Department until the surrender of General R. E. Lee at Appomattox. Returned to Baltimore August 1865.

JAMES McNULTY

Born at Baltimore. Enlisted May 1861 at Harpers Ferry as a private in Company D, First Maryland Infantry. Discharged at Centerville, VA, December 1861 for disability. I was captured at Hagerstown, MD, July 7, 1863. Taken to Old Capitol Prison, Washington, DC. Then taken to and tried at Berlin, MD, for being a spy. Sentenced to be hung. Reprieved by General Patrick and returned to old Capitol Prison. Keep in close confinement for about one year, then sent to Point Lookout. Exchanged March 1865. Reported to Admiral Buchanan and was placed in charge of Ordnance sent from Richmond to Salisbury, NC, (prison) when General Bradley T. Johnson was in command.

GEORGE LAVENDER McGUIRE

Born at Carollton, GA. Enlisted July 1861 near Manassas, VA, in Company A, "Rome Light Guards," Eighth Georgia Infantry as a private. In the following engagements: Seven Days Battles in front of Richmond, Second Battle of Manassas, Sharpsburg and Fredericksburg. Discharged June 6, 1863, near Culpeper, VA.

WILLIAM THOMAS MORGAN

Born in Matthews County, VA. Enlisted in September 1861 at Matthews County Court House First Corporal Company D, Armistead's Artillery. Term of service for the duration of the war. In the following engagements: Yorktown, Little Bethel, Deep Bottom, Bottom's Bridge, Cold Harbor, Wilderness and all the other actions in which my command was engaged. Surrendered at Appomattox, VA.

JOHN CRAIG MONTGOMERY

Born at Baltimore City July 20, 1842. Enlisted at Heathville, VA, January 1862 as a private in the Chesapeake Battery (Fourth Maryland Artillery) for one year. Discharged January 1863 on expiration of term of service and sickness. In the battles of Seven Days before Richmond, Cedar Mountain, Harpers Ferry, Second Manassas, Fredericksburg. Never took the oath or paroled.

JAMES MAHONEY

Born in King George County, VA. Enlisted August 1, 1861, at Matthias Point on the Potomac River as a private in Purcell's Battery, Pegram's Battalion for three years. Re-enlisted at Fredericksburg in the same command. Wounded by a fragment of shell in the left thigh during Seven Days fight in front of Richmond. Wounded again at Gettysburg when a piece of shell broke my ankle. In the following battles: Wilderness, Gettysburg, Fredericksburg, Petersburg, Seven Pines and others in which my battery was engaged. Paroled at King George County Court House after the surrender of General Lee.

PETER HENRY McCLEERY

Born in Alleghany County (now Garrett), MD. Lived in Hagerstown in 1858. Enlisted at Martinsburg April 20, 1862, as a private in Company C, First

Maryland Cavalry. Re-enlisted in same company April 1863 at Winchester for the war. Participated in all battles and actions my command was engaged in during the war. Paroled at Winchester May 1865.

RICHARD NEWTON MCVEIGH

Born at Middleburg, Loudoun County, VA, on January 5, 1828. Enlisted at Huntsville, AL, in Colonel Coltant's Regiment, Captain Gaston's Company at the outbreak of the war where I remained about a month when I was transferred to a Mississippi regiment. Went with this regiment to Pensacola, FL, where I remained until Virginia seceded. Then I came on to Virginia and joined an Alabama regiment and had our headquarters at Hot Springs and Martinsburg. We were then acting as scouts for General Joseph E. Johnson when we went with him to Manassas and was in the First Battle of Bull Run fight. Shortly after this I was mustered out of this command and joined Mosby where I remained until the end of the war. Wounded several times—with a saber through the breast and a gunshot wound. Was a prisoner of war at the Old Capitol (Prison) in Washington, DC. At Lee's surrender at Appomattox Court House and was paroled by order of General U. S. Grant.

Author's note: Most of this does not seem possible.

GEORGE DOUGLASS MCCLURE

Born at Bunker Hill, Berkeley County, VA, February 25, 1840. Enlisted March 1862 at Fort Lowery on the Rappahannock River in the Chesapeake Battery, Captain Forest in command, where I remained during the war. Cedar Mountain was the first engagement I was in. Then came Harpers Ferry, the Second battle of Manassas, Fredericksburg, Chancellorsville, Winchester, Gettysburg. When we fell back from Pennsylvania was ordered to the Wilderness. After that was ordered to take position on the south side of Fort Gregg. This was the last stand taken around Petersburg when we surrendered two days before General Lee surrendered at Appomattox Court House. I was paroled with Lee's army.

THOMAS H. MACKEN

Was born in Matthews County, VA, May 3, 1842. Enlisted in the "King and Queen" Cavalry (Captain M. P. Todd commanding) for one year in June 1861 at Gloucester Point, VA. Re-enlisted in same company in 1862 near Seven Pines. Captured once near Catoctin Furnace, MD, on September 13, 1862. Exchanged December 1862. Was in all the battles my command was engaged in. Wounded October 23, 1863, at Morton's Ford on the Rapidan. Laid down my arms after General Lee surrendered at Appomattox.

ALBANO RUTLEDGE MILES

Was born in Middlesex County, VA, October 15, 1845. Enlisted as a private in Lee's Virginia Rangers, Company H, Ninth Virginia Cavalry in 1864. I remained in this command during the war. In the fights around Petersburg received gunshot wound in the left hand disabling it for life. Never captured.

DENNIS T. MADIGAN

Born in New York, NY, December 3, 1833. Enlisted in the Richmond Howitzers April 1861 where I served a short time. Then re-enlisted in Captain Hayward's Company, Colonel Brown's Battalion of Cavalry where I served about two years when I was detailed as courier for General G.W.C. Lee where I remained until General Lee surrendered at Appomattox. Never captured. Was slightly wounded in the hand when my horse was killed in a skirmish the night before the battle of Yellow Tavern. Paroled in Richmond at the end of the war.

WILLIAM WATTS MOORE

Born in Jamesville, Martin County, NC, on October 28, 1844. Enlisted for the war as a private in Company H, First North Carolina Infantry at Williamston, Martin County, NC, on February 2, 1862. Remained with same command until General R. E. Lee surrendered at Appomattox Court House. Was in all the engagements that my command was in. Never wounded. Captured at Strasburg, VA, October 1864 and escaped the same day.

CLARENCE HENRY MACKUBIN

Born in Baltimore April 17, 1837. Enlisted as a private in Company K, First Virginia Cavalry at Culpeper, VA, November 1862. I served in this command till the close of the war. Participated in the battles of Chancellorsville, Gettysburg, and Cold Harbor. Never wounded. Captured near Harpers Ferry in the fall of 1864 and carried to Elmira, NY, and there incarcerated where I remained until the close of the war.

JAMES McDOWELL

Born at Aberdeen, Scotland 1831. Enlisted at New Mexico in Feal's Artillery, Libbey's Brigade, in which I served during the war. Never a prisoner. Was engaged in the battles of Alverda, Fort Filmor, Abereurke and numerous other engagements in Arizona, Mosses Lane and Mainsfield in Texas, Camp Beashy in Louisiana and Franklin Court House. At the re-taking of Galveston. Then transferred to gunboats *Mary Hill* and *Webb* until the end of the war. Never a prisoner or paroled.

CORNELIUS SAXTON MULLIN

Born in Baltimore November 14, 1843. Enlisted as a private in Captain Rasin's Company, First Maryland Cavalry of the Maryland Line in which command remained during the entire war. Was captured whilst scouting near Front Royal about the first of May 1863. Was carried to Fort McHenry near Baltimore where I remained some 2 weeks. Then exchanged and returned to my command then stationed in the valley of Virginia. Never wounded. Was laid up with

Rheumatism when General Robert E. Lee surrendered at Appomattox Court House.

JAMES MONAHAN

Born in Ireland, don't know when. Enlisted as a private in the fall of 1861 at Richmond in the Baltimore Light Artillery. Left this command in the summer of 1862 when I enlisted in Major T. Sturgess Davis' command of cavalry, Imboden's Brigade which operated in the Valley and West Virginia. Remained in this command until General R. E. Lee surrendered. Never wounded. Captured once during a raid in the Valley and re-captured after being half an hour a prisoner in the hands of the Yankees. Surrendered with the command at Winchester shortly after the army under General R. E. Lee surrendered at Appomattox Court House on April 9, 1865.

THOMAS BRUMLEY MARTIN

Born in King William County, VA, September 8, 1845. Enlisted as second lieutenant in Stonewall Artillery, Local Defense of Virginia at King and Queen Court House August 1862. Served in this command till September 8, 1863, when I resigned my commission and re-enlisted as a private in Company F, Twenty-fourth Virginia Cavalry in which command I served until the end of the war. Was paroled May 6, 1865. Captured in King and Queen County, VA, by Kilpatrick's Cavalry—they being on a raid. Only remained a prisoner in their hands about six hours making my escape from them when night came on. Never wounded.

ROBERT CARTER NICHOLAS

Born at Richmond January 12, 1839. Enlisted 1861 at Richmond as a private in Company F, Fifty-ninth Virginia Regiment Infantry, Wise's Brigade, for the war. Was promoted to orderly sergeant which I held for two years, then captain of the company until a prisoner at Danville when war ended. Was in numerous engagements in West Virginia, battles in front of Petersburg. Also on the islands around Charleston, SC.

CHARLES AUGUSTINE NEWTON

Born at Alexandria, VA, February 28, 1844. Enlisted at Norfolk May 10, 1861, in Company G, Sixth Virginia Regiment in which I served nine months at Craney Island. Re-enlisted May 1862 for the war in Grandy's Battery (Norfolk Light Artillery Blues) at Petersburg. Took part in battles of Fredericksburg, Chancellorsville, Gettysburg, Wilderness, Cold Harbor, and defense of Petersburg. Wounded at Petersburg in Fort Mahone August 13, 1864, losing my left leg and receiving a discharge from the service.

CHARLES NOLL

Entered in the Confederate Army May 10, 1861, as a private in Company K, Brook's and Rhett's Battery of Artillery, Second South Carolina Regiment. Was in the engagements of First Manassas, Chickahominy, Mechanicsville, Gaines' Mills, Frazer's Farm, First Cold Harbor, White Oak Swamp, Malvern Hill, Second Manassas, Sharpsburg, Fredericksburg, Chancellorsville and Gettysburg. Was wounded at Battle of Gettysburg where I was taken prisoner and incarcerated at Point Lookout where I remained until General Lee surrendered.

Enlisted in the Brook's Guards Company K, Second South Carolina Regiment for one year by permission of the Secretary of War. The company re-enlisted February 2, 1862, near Centerville, VA, and changed the branch of service to that of Light Artillery. "Amongst whom there was no better or braver soldier than Charles Noll. He stood ready and willing for every call." This was signed by his first lieutenant and sergeant.

FRANCIS FLETCHER NELSON

Born Snow Hill, Worcester County, MD, May 4, 1835. Enlisted as a private in Snowden Andrews First Maryland Light Artillery about July 1861 at Richmond. I remained in this command three years and three months when I was honorably discharged. Never re-enlisted owing to a serious injury received in the right wrist. Received a flesh wound at Second Manassas August 28, 1862. Sent to hospital at Middleburg, Loudoun County where I remained only a week when a gentleman—a stranger to me, came to the hospital and carried me with him to his home where I remained six months and then reported back to my command then stationed at Bowling Green. Whilst lying wounded in this gentleman's home a squad of Federals came along and captured me and paroled me on the spot. If I had not been wounded and on crutches think they would have carried me off with them.

BENJAMIN WELCH OWENS

Born in Anne Arundel County, MD. Enlisted for the war at Richmond May 1863 as a private in the First Maryland Artillery. Received a scratch wound on shoulder at battle of Gettysburg and had my foot painfully mashed by a grape shot June 22, 1864, in front of Petersburg, but not sufficiently injured to render it necessary to go to the hospital. In June 1863 was engaged in the battles of Winchester and Stephenson's Depot and subsequently at Gettysburg, Bristow Station, and Mine Run. In 1864 at Totlopottomey Creek, Turkey Ridge, and Cold Harbor and through the siege of Petersburg from June 18 to some time in October. On account of illness was sent to Robertson's Hospital. After improvement reported ready for my command, but was pronounced by Board of Examining Surgeons unfit and recommended for light duty. Ordered to report to Major Corneluis Boyle, Provost Marshal and Commandant of the post at Gordonsville. Was assigned to duty as clerk at his Headquarters. Remained there until the surrender of General R. E. Lee and his army. Proceeding to Washington, DC, after being paroled in Richmond. Was arrested and informed that an order had been issued by the Secretary of War that those that had entered the Confederate service from the Loyal States. Not withstanding their parole, should not be permitted to return to their homes without subscribing to the Oath of Allegiance. Declining this was imprisoned in Alexandria, VA, until after the surrender of all Confederate forces. Paroled at Richmond April 14 or 15, 1865.

Benjamin Franklin Pitts

Born at Eagles Nest, Caroline County, VA. Settled in Maryland in 1846. Enlisted June 12,1861 at Culpeper Court House as a private in Company E, Seventh Virginia Infantry. Was taken prisoner the latter part of March or the first part of April 1865 and confined at Point Lookout. Was in the following named battles: Bull Run, First Manassas, Williamsburg, Seven Pines, Frazier's Farm, Plymouth, NC, Drewry's Bluff, Fredericksburg, Gettysburg, Five Forks, Sailor's Creek, Second Manassas, and many other skirmishes. Was released from Point Lookout May 10, 1865.

Charles Richard Price

Born in Alexandria, VA. From July 1861 to the spring of 1862 acted as orderly in the Commissary Department of Major Fowel. Then I enlisted at Richmond as a private in Company A, Thirty-first Virginia Battalion. Was detailed to duty in the Friction Primer Department on Belle Island. Remained in that department until the time of my service had expired. Then re-enlisted May 1863 at Richmond as a private in Company H, Seventeenth Virginia Infantry for the war. Was in the following named battles: Cold Harbor, Drewry's Bluff, Howlet's House, Dinwiddie Court House, Five Forks, Frazier's Farm, Darbytown Road, and many skirmishes. When war over went to Lynchburg.

William Henry Pope

Born in Frederick City, MD, February 14, 1843. Enlisted for one year July 25, 1861, as a private in Company A (a Frederick company), First Maryland Infantry C.S.A. at Fairfax Court House. Re-enlisted at Fairfax Station January 1862 in the same company and regiment for the war. Was promoted to corporal and then sergeant. Was discharged August 17, 1862, at Gordonsville by General Orders. Re-enlisted for the war in April 1863 at Lacey's Spring, VA, as a private in Company D, First Maryland Cavalry. Was taken prisoner near Hagerstown, MD, on July 5, 1863. Was confined in Fort McHenry, Fort Delaware, and Point Lookout. Was exchanged December 25, 1863. Was wounded on the left lower rib by a musket ball at the battle of Gaines' Mills June 27, 1862, and by a pistol ball in the left hand at Hagerstown July 5, 1863. Was paroled May 23, 1865, at Harpers Ferry. Participated in fifty-nine battles and skirmishes. Was elected Superintendent of the Maryland Line Confederate Home April 1888.

Ephriam Howard Poole

Born in Frederick County, MD. Served in the Medical Department of C.S.A. under Dr. James T. Johnson in the spring of 1862. Remained with Dr. Johnson until I enlisted in 1863 in an infantry company at Salisbury, NC, as a private for the protection of Medical Stores, etc, etc, at the later place. Paroled at Salisbury, NC, after General Johnson's surrender.

HENRY PYFER

Born at Exchange Place, Baltimore City, February 14, 1845. Enlisted December 1, 1862, at Winchester in Company A, Second Maryland Infantry in which command I served until General Lee surrendered at Appomattox. Was in all the battles that my command was engaged in. Captured near Petersburg April 1865. Carried to Point Lookout Prison about three weeks or until Lee surrendered when I was released. Never surrendered.

ALONZO JENKINS PITTMAN

Born in New Bern, NC, November 1844. Enlisted in Company B, Sixty-seventh North Carolina infantry as a private in the spring of 1862 in which command I remained until the close of the war. Never captured. Slightly wounded by a minnie ball in the wrist in skirmish in the vicinity of New Bern. Paroled after General Lee surrendered.

CHARLES PENDERGRASS

Born in Baltimore January 4, 1836. Enlisted as a private at New Orleans, LA, 1861 in Company C, First Special Battalion where I remained 16 months when the command was disbanded. I was in the first battle of Manassas where I was wounded in the leg "gun shot." Then Gaines' Mill. Was wounded in all three times. All "gun shot" wounds and in the leg three times. When my command was disbanded I entered the Laboratory in Richmond as a workman where I remained till the end of the war when I was paroled.

JAMES EDWARD PRICE

Born September 8, 1844, in Baltimore County, MD. Enlisted as a private in Company D, First Maryland Cavalry at Winchester, VA, about October 1, 1862. In this command I remained till the war closed or the surrender of Gen. Robert E. Lee April 9, 1865, at Appomattox Court House. Received slight gunshot wound in the head at the battle of Haw's Shop, VA, June 18, 1864. Was sent to the Chimborazo Hospital where I remained five or six weeks when I reported back to the command for duty having recovered from the wound. Captured near Strasburg, VA, March 1865. Taken to Winchester, then to Harpers Ferry. There paroled about two weeks before General Lee surrendered and came home to Maryland.

MICHAEL ALOYSIOUS QUINN

Born in Baltimore 27th day of July 1844. Enlisted at Harpers Ferry 22nd of May 1861 as a private in Company E, First Maryland Regiment Infantry. Was appointed Musician in October of the same year and was in every skirmish and battle that the regiment was engaged in. Was mustered with the regiment at

Gordonsville on the 17th day of August 1862. Never was a prisoner. Re-enlisted at Richmond 27th day of August 1862 as a private in Company A, Second Maryland Infantry. Was again appointed Musician at Hanover Junction on 28th day of December 1863 to rank as such from the first day of July previous to the battle of Gettysburg. Was with the command on every march and engagement. Whilst with the Second Regiment in front of Petersburg met and talked to my father who was a member of the Second Maryland Infantry in the Federal Army. This occurred on the lines at the front. I was mustered out with the few that was left of the Second Maryland Regiment C.S.A. at Appomattox Court House on the 9th of April 1865.

JOHN HENRY SKINNER QUYNN

Born February 3, 1842, in Notingham, Prince George's County, MD. Enlisted for the war in Company E, First Maryland Cavalry in 1862. Served in this command until the expiration of the war. Never wounded. Ran the blockade in the fall of 1864 with a comrade in the fall of 1864—Edward Rich. Came to Baltimore where we were both captured, court martialled, and sentenced to be hung. However this sentence was commuted to imprisonment. We were then both of us on to Fort Delaware Prison where we remained until General Robert E. Lee surrendered at Appomattox. Was in the battles of Gettysburg, and Winchester and many skirmishes. The first fight I was in was at Greenland Gap.

JOHN RILEY

Born in County Dublin, Ireland. Enlisted August 22, 1861, at Shreveport, LA, as a private in Company K, Eleventh Louisiana Infantry. Was transferred August 17, 1863, to Company G, Fifth Louisiana Infantry. Was wounded May 5, 1864, at the Battle of the Wilderness. Was made prisoner and sent to the Lincoln Hospital at Washington, DC. Then to old Capitol Prison. On the 2nd of January 1865 was sent to Elmira, NY, for special exchange of wounded prisoners. Was exchanged at City Point on 11th of February 1865 and sent to the Louisiana Hospital. Was wounded in the side at Tupelo, TN. Was in the following named battles: Belmont, MO, Island No. 10, New Madrid, MO, Fort Pillow, Corinth, MS, Shiloh, Tupelo, Mine Run, Bristoe Station, Wilderness, and many skirmishes. Was paroled at Richmond April 17, 1865.

DR. FENWICK ROBERTSON

Born Kingston, Somerset County, MD. Was appointed Assistant Surgeon May 1863 at Richmond and assigned to Jackson Hospital where I remained until 1865 when paroled.

JOHN DUHAMEL RICHARDSON

Born in Queen Anne County, MD. Enlisted October 1862 in the Fourth Maryland "Chesapeake" Artillery for the war at Richmond as a private. Then promoted to sergeant. Engaged in the battles of Wilderness, Fredericksburg,

Gettysburg, and others. I surrendered 12 men and one gun at Appomattox Court House April 1865.

JOHN CHARLES RYAN

Born at Baltimore. Enlisted in Charleston, SC, as a private January 14, 1861, in Company B, First South Carolina Artillery for the term of one year. Re-enlisted at Fort Sumter November 1862 in the same company for the war. Was in all the engagements around Charleston with my company. Taken prisoner at the battle of Bentonville, NC. Taken to Point Lookout, then to Washington, DC, and there paroled in July 1865.

JOHN DANIEL RIORDAN

Born in Limerick County, Ireland. Enlisted at Harpers Ferry April 1861 as a private in the Wise Artillery for one year. After serving 15 months re-enlisted in the same command for the war. Was in the battles of First Manassas, Yorktown, Williamsburg, Seven Days before Richmond, Chancellorsville, and all actions in which my command was engaged. Paroled at Richmond after the surrender at Appomattox.

JAMES ALOYSIUS RYAN

Born in Frederick County, MD, on November 25, 1835. Enlisted as a private in Company H, First Maryland Regiment of Infantry at Richmond June 19, 1861. In which command I served 12 months when the company was mustered out of service—its time expired. In January 1863 I re-enlisted again as a private in Captain Breathed's Battery of General J.E.B. Stuart's Horse Artillery in Richmond. In this command I remained till General R. E. Lee surrendered at Appomattox Court House. Received a slight flesh wound at the Second Battle of Cold Harbor. Captured in September 1864 at the battle of Fisher's Hill. Was incarcerated in the prison at Point Lookout where I remained until General R. E. Lee surrendered at Appomattox Court House.

RICHARD TYLER REYNOLDS

Born in Westmorland County, VA, May 20, 1844. Enlisted as a private April 1862 at Heathsville in Company C, Fortieth Virginia Regiment of Infantry in which command I remained until the expiration of the war. Was in all the battles that my command engaged in whilst I was with it. Wounded slightly in the head by a minie ball at the battle of Cold Harbor near Richmond in July 1862. Captured whilst skirmishing in the summer of 1863. Carried to Point Lookout Prison. I was exchanged after 3 months imprisonment here. Then joined my command and remained until it surrendered at Appomattox Court House. Then paroled and returned home.

HENRY SCHULTZ

Born in Germany. Left Baltimore City for Charleston, SC, February 28, 1861. Enlisted in Company B, First South Carolina Regulars as a private.

Afterwards transferred to Company D, First South Carolina Infantry as a drill sergeant. Then promoted to first sergeant. Wounded at Fort Wagner, SC, July 1863 in the shoulder by a bayonet stab, also by sword cut. Wounded at Sullivan's Island by a piece of shell in the back. In the battles of Fort Wagner, Sullivan's Island, James Island, Jones Island, and the siege of Fort Sumter and at the surrender of Major Anderson USA. At Fort Moultrie and Battery Marshal I sighted the 10-inch gun that killed 14 men in 1863.

EDWARD ADOLPHUS SHEEKS

Born at Baltimore City. Enlisted June 1862 at Knoxville, TN, in Company D, Second Kentucky Cavalry as a private. Captured at Mt. Sterling, KY. Taken to Cincinnati, then to Camp Chase and finally to Johnson's Island where I remained 10 months. Paroled May 12, 1865. In battles of Chickamauga, McElmore's Cove, Bean's Station and other actions in which my command was engaged.

ELHANNAN COLLIA SMITH

Born in Baltimore City. Enlisted May 1863 at Richmond as a private in Company D, Second Virginia Infantry. Was in the battles of Drewry's Bluff, Seven Pines, Yellow Tavern, Dahlgren's Raid, Fort Gilmor, and all the actions in which my command was engaged. Was paroled in Chesterfield County, VA, April 1865.

JOSEPH CARBERRY SANNER

Born in Saint Mary's County, MD. Enlisted April 1861 at Portsmouth, VA, in Company C, Sixteenth Virginia Infantry. Promoted to orderly sergeant. We were stationed on the Norfolk side of the Elizabeth River for over one year. After Norfolk City was evacuated, the regiment proceeded to Richmond and then to Gordonsville. Having re-enlisted again an election was had for officers. After the election there was dissatisfaction at the result. I ask to be transferred to the Maryland Line and reported to Major Kyle at Richmond. I met Colonel H.T. Parrish who had been elected Colonel of the Sixteenth Virginia Infantry who advised me to raise a company for Brigadier General Floyd who was then in West Virginia. The recruits were to be volunteers and not liable to conscription. In the event I did so Colonel Parrish was to procure me a commission from Governor Letcher. I soon found it impossible. I then went to work at the Navy Yard where they needed men—I being a ship's joiner. The men in the different departments formed a battalion, Major Carlin commanding. We were ordered out at all the raids made by the enemy—Stoneman's, Dahlgren's, and others. In front of Fort Harrison we had a very lively skirmish. The enemy at the time occupied the fort. I was at the Navy yard until the evacuation of Richmond.

BENJAMIN BUSHROD SPICER

Born in Warren County, VA June 23, 1833. Enlisted in May 1861 at Front Royal, VA, as a private in Company E, Seventh Virginia Cavalry in which command I remained till General R. E. Lee surrendered at Appomattox Court House. I participated in all battles and skirmishes my command "Rosser's Laurel Brigade" was engaged in which were very numerous and all over the Valley and other parts of Virginia. Never wounded or captured. The command surrendered at Appomattox April 9, 1865.

FREDERICK AUGUSTA STEWART

Born at Baltimore City. Enlisted May 1862 at Moorfield, Hardy County, VA, as a private in McNeill's Rangers. Served all the war through. Paroled May 19, 1865, at Cumberland, MD. Wounded in the hip by fragments of shell at Charlestown, WV. Wounded, saber cut in the head at Moorefield. Wounded, saber cut on hand at Harrisonburg. Wounded by a pistol ball in the side at Williamsport. Assisted in the capture of generals Crook and Kelly at Cumberland. Participated in battles of New Market, Gettysburg, Frederick, Monocacy, Winchester, and all the battles and skirmishes in which my command was engaged.

HENRY FREDERICK SLEEPACK

Born at Washington, DC, on January 3, 1837. Shortly after my birth my parents located in the city of Baltimore where I resided until commencement of Civil War. I then proceeded to Richmond and enlisted for one year as a private in Company C, First Maryland Regiment Infantry. This was on the 18th day of June 1861. Was honorably discharged at Staunton, VA, August 1862, time of service having expired. Was taken prisoner and confined at Point Lookout until the early summer of 1863. Was then exchanged with a number of others and sent to Richmond where shortly afterwards I re-enlisted in the Third Virginia Battalion of Infantry. Remained with this command until Richmond was evacuated. I then tried to join the Army of the Mississippi, but was stopped at Salisbury, NC, and fully convinced the war was over. Returned to Richmond and was paroled June 1865. Was in all engagements my command took part in.

BEDINGFIELD HAND SPENCER

Born in Kent County, MD. Enlisted spring of 1862 at Richmond as a private in the Chesapeake Battery, Fourth Maryland Artillery for 3 years. Re-enlisted in same command for the war. Participated in both battles of Fredericksburg, Sharpsburg, Harpers Ferry, Gettysburg, and all other actions in which my command was engaged. Paroled at Appomattox when General Lee surrendered.

THOMAS SUNDERLAND

Born in Calvert County, MD. Enlisted August 1862 at Brook's Station, VA, as a private in the First Maryland Artillery for the war. Wounded in the eye by a minie ball at White Oak Swamp. In battles of Cold Harbor, Seven Pines, Petersburg, and others in which my command was engaged. Detailed in Medical Department on account of my wound for about fifteen months. Discharged at Richmond in the fall of 1864 for disability.

GEORGE BARNHARDT SCHILLING

Born December 14, 1813, at Hanover, Germany. Enlisted April 1861 at Keysville, VA, as a corporal in Company K, Twenty-third Virginia Regiment for the war. Was never a prisoner. Served through the Valley Campaign and all other actions in which the Army of Northern Virginia was engaged. As a corporal was detailed as Hospital Steward at Staunton, VA. Paroled at Richmond after the army surrendered.

THOMAS RICHARD STEWART

Born in Dorchester County, MD, November 23, 1830. Enlisted October 31, 1862, as a private in Company G, Second Maryland Regiment Infantry for the war. In November 1862 elected first lieutenant of Company G. Promoted captain January 26, 1863. In the battles of Winchester, Gettysburg, and all other engagements with my command. Paroled at Augusta, GA in 1865. Prior to my enlisting was pilot on York River from July 1861 to the evacuation of Yorktown. Was a prisoner in Old Capitol Prison at Washington, DC from May 1861 to latter part of June 1861. Wounded at Gettysburg severely in the ankle and a slight wound in the head. Was then assigned to General John H. Winder at the Passport Office in Richmond. From there to Camp Lawton in charge of Prisoners and then to Columbia, SC, under Major Griswold.

GEORGE STRAIN

Born in Jefferson County, VA. Enlisted June 7, 1864, at Petersburg in Company C, Eighteenth Virginia Battalion Infantry for one year. Re-enlisted same company and regiment for the war at No. 9 Battery. Prison on retreat from Petersburg. Captured between latter place and Appomattox. Battles: Seven Pines in which was wounded in leg, Darbytown Road, Dahlgren's Raid, etc. Paroled at Washington, DC, April 1865.

JOSEPH COSMAS SHORT

Was born at Emmittsburg, Frederick County, MD, on April 30, 1843. Enlisted in the fall of 1861 in General Hardee's No. 4 Heavy Artillery where I served for one year. Was then transferred to Company F, First Maryland Cavalry where I remained until Lee surrendered. Was in all the engagements my command was in. Never wounded and never captured. Took the oath and paroled in Richmond May 1865.

ROBERT SELDEN SMITH

Born in Fauquier County, VA, February 17, 1844. Enlisted in A. D. Smith's Company M of Infantry October 5, 1861. This company was disbanded March 15, 1862. Then I re-enlisted under Colonel Ashby, that famous Virginian cavalryman, for the war as a private at Currenstown, VA. This was on March 22, 1862. Ashby then commanded Company A, Seventh Virginia Cavalry which was in General Rosser's "Laurel Brigade." I was in all engagements that my command was in and served in it until the close of the war. Received a slight gunshot wound in the arm near the elbow during the summer of 1863 near Cedar Run in the Valley of Virginia. Never captured.

John Capron Snowden

Born in Prince George's County, MD, June 29, 1843. Enlisted in Virginia as a private in Company C, First Maryland Cavalry June 1, 1863. Remained in this command until General Robert E. Lee surrendered at Appomattox. Was engaged in the battles of Pollard's Farm, Kernstown, Winchester, Williamsport, Brandy Station, Gettysburg, and was specially detailed to accompany Colonel Harry Gilmor on his famous raid into Maryland when General Jubal Early made that dash into Maryland and got very close to Washington City. Also at the burning of Chambersburg and many cavalry skirmishes. Was captured at Moorefield, WV, when the Yanks made a dash on that place. Imprisoned at Camp Chase, OH, where I remained until a few days before the fall of Richmond. Was then paroled and exchanged. Never wounded.

Hugh Alexander Southerd

Born in Caroline County, VA, January 5, 1840. Enlisted as a private in Company E, Thirtieth Virginia Regiment of Infantry on May 21, 1861. In this command I remained until badly wounded at the battle of Drewry's Bluff, May 16, 1864, when I was sent to Chimborazo Hospital in Richmond where I remained till General Robert E. Lee surrendered at Appomattox Court House. Received a flesh wound through the face at the battle of Seven Pines. My command was in service several months in North Carolina and helped to capture the town of Plymouth in that state in the year 1864. Never a prisoner of war.

James Monroe Swann

Born in Caroline County, VA, February 26, 1843. Enlisted as a private in Company E, Fourteenth Virginia Regiment of Infantry in Richmond on May 12, 1861. In this command I served till General Robert E. Lee surrendered at Appomattox Court House. Received gun shot—shrapnel slight wound left knee in Pickett's famous charge at Gettysburg July 3, 1863. But not sufficiently severe to prevent from keeping me following my command up to turning the enemies' guns on themselves. Engaged in the following named battles: Seven Pines June 1, 1862, Frazier's Farm June 30, 1862, Malvern Hill July 1, 1862, Second Manassas August 28–30, 1862, Harpers Ferry September 16, 1862, Sharpsburg September 17, 1862, Fredericksburg December 13, 1862, Suffolk February 10, 1863, Drewry's Bluff May 16, 1864, and numerous other smaller fights. Never captured. Surrendered at Appomattox Court House April 9, 1865.

Dewitt Clinton Sears

Born in state of New York January 1843. Enlisted as a private in the Richmond Howitzers at Richmond in July of 1862. In this command I remained till the surrender of General Robert E. Lee at Appomattox Court House April 9, 1865. Was in all the battles my battery was engaged in—Fredericksburg, Chancellorsville, Gettysburg, and many others up to the siege and the many bloody battles fought around Petersburg. Never a prisoner of war nor wounded. Surrendered with General Lee at Appomattox.

RICHARD BOSWELL STUBBS

Born in Baltimore City February 14, 1836. Enlisted as a private in the Eighteenth Regiment of Infantry of Tennessee, Company G, at Nashville on April 21, 1861. Served in this command the entire war and was with the command when it surrendered with General Joseph E. Johnson at High Point, NC in April 1865. Was wounded in the right leg at Fort Donelson, TN. Bone badly fractured by a minie ball February 21, 1863. The whole brigade, General Buckner's surrendered on this occasion. I among the number to General Smith, the Federal commander. We were prisoners of war 7 months at Camp Butler, IL. We were exchanged and sent to Vicksburg, MS. The brigade was then sent to Murfreesboro, TN to join General Joseph E. Johnson's command and remained with him till close of the war. When I first enlisted in the regiment it was for 90 days in the Tennessee State troops. When the state seceded early in 1861 the command was mustered in for the war. Am suffering badly now from the old wound.

THOMAS HEBER SNOWDEN

Born January 28, 1845, at Edenton, NC. Enlisted as a private in Captain S. Marin's Battery, Twelfth Virginia Light Artillery. Enlisted for the war. Served in this command 18 months when I was transferred to the Thirteenth North Carolina Light Artillery commanded by Captain L. H. Webb in which command remained till close of the war. I was in all the battles that my two different commands participated in. Never captured. Never wounded.

CHARLES HENRY TAYLOR

Born in Loraine County, OH. Enlisted January 4, 1861, in Company A, First Louisiana Regulars at New Orleans. Discharged April 1861. Re-enlisted May 4, 1861, in Company E, Fifth Louisiana Infantry as a private. Wounded by a minnie ball in the leg. At the Second battle of Fredericksburg, captured on the Rappahannock River, but escaped the first night after being a prisoner. In 37 general engagements, also many skirmishes. Paroled April 11, 1865.

JOHN WILLIAM THOMPSON

Born in Saint Mary's County, MD. Enlisted June 16, 1861, as a private at Tappahannock, VA, in Company H, First Maryland Zouaves. October 1862 re-enlisted in Company G, Second Maryland Infantry. Taken prisoner at Amelia Springs, VA, April 7, 1865, and sent to Point Lookout. Released July 11, 1865—war ended. Was in the following battles: Yorktown, Williamsburg, Seven

Pines, Winchester, Cold Harbor, Weldon Railroad, Squirrel Level Road, Gettysburg, Hatcher's Run, and other actions with my regiment.

THOMAS MASKINS THOMPSON

Born in Saint Mary's County, MD, April 1, 1836. Enlisted June 1861 at Richmond as a private in Company I, First Maryland Infantry Regiment for one year. Re-enlisted August 1862 in the First Maryland Artillery at Charlottesville for the war. Never a prisoner. Was engaged in the following battles and skirmishes: Valley Campaign, Gettysburg, Yellow Tavern, and all other battles and skirmishes that the Army of Northern Virginia was engaged in. Was paroled after the surrender at Lynchburg, VA.

CHARLES EDWARD TERRES

Born in Philadelphia, PA, February 1836. Raised in Charlotte, NC. Enlisted for the war in Captain John R. Erwin's Company F, Fifth North Carolina Cavalry in August 1862 as a private. Elected third lieutenant in said company in 1863. In the battles of Reams Station, Malvern Hill, Brandy Station, Wilderness, Five Forks. Discharged at Danville, VA April 14, 1865, by General John C. Breckenridge.

MAXIMULLIAN ALAWAY KEPLER TIPPITT

Was born in St. Mary's County, MD, December 11, 1835. Enlisted about the last of July 1862 in Company B, First Maryland Cavalry under Colonel Ridgley Brown. Served in this command until the close of the war. Was captured at Cedar Creek in September 1863. Was carried to Camp Chase, OH, where I was paroled and sent to Richmond just one week before the surrender at Appomattox. Participated in all the engagements that my command was in. Was never wounded.

LEONIDAS JOSEPH TEARNEY

Born in Hagerstown, MD, February 12, 1827. Enlisted as a private in Company D, Twelfth Virginia Regiment of Cavalry of Rosser's Laurel Brigade on July 1, 1863. At Brandy Station. I remained in this command until General Robert E. Lee surrendered at Appomattox Court House on April 9, 1865. My first engagement was the celebrated Battle of Brandy Station where Rosser's Brigade opened the fight early in the morning. Was engaged in most of the battles my command participated in. Never wounded. Had two horses killed under me in different battles. Captured at Smithfield, VA, in a cavalry skirmish, but only remained a prisoner about half-hour when I made my escape in the confusion that ensued from a charge and counter-charge.

HEZEKIAH WILLIAM VEIRS

Born Montgomery County, MD, March 21, 1824. Enlisted August 1862 at Edinburg, Shenandoah Valley, VA, in Company B, White's Battalion of Cavalry for the war. Captured at Brandy Station June 9, 1863. Prisoner about two months in Old Capitol Prison, Washington, DC. Never paroled. In the following battles and actions: Brandy Station, Culpeper, Chancellorsville, Wilderness, Seven Days around Richmond, on retreat from Richmond to Appomattox, Cedar Creek, and all other actions when scouting on the border of the Potomac River. Slight wound in forehead at High Bridge on retreat of our army. Wound in hip by fragment of shell at the Wilderness.

NICHOLAS W. WATKINS

Born in Baltimore City March 9, 1841. Enlisted September 1862 at Old Fair Grounds of Hagerstown, MD, as a private in Company H, Ninth Georgia Infantry for the war, Anderson's Brigade, Hood's Division, Longstreet's Corps. Was transferred to the Baltimore Light Artillery in November 1864. Was the only one of my command to surrender with General Lee at Appomattox. Was in the following battles: Bristoe Station, Sharpsburg, Fredericksburg, the operation around Suffolk, Lynchburg and Hunters Raid, Gettysburg, Campbell's Station in East Tennessee, Siege of Knoxville including the charge on Fort Saunders, Petersburg and Appomattox.

LOUIS CLINTON WAGGENER

Born in Baltimore City August 23, 1843. Enlisted at Portsmouth, VA, in May 1862 as a private in Company E, Sixty-first Virginia Infantry, Mahone's Brigade, Anderson's Division, A. P. Hill's Corps. While acting as rear guard two days before the surrender of General Lee, was taken prisoner and sent to Point Lookout where I remained until July 1865. Was in the following named battles: Fredericksburg, Chancellorsville, Second Cold Harbor, Spotsylvania Court House, Wilderness, Crater, Ream's Station, Weldon Railroad, Buger's Mill, Hatcher's Run and all the battles in front of Petersburg.

DOUGLAS AUGUSTUS WITHERS

Born in Stafford County, VA. Enlisted June 1861 at Fredericksburg as a private in Company G, Fortieth Virginia Infantry. Was wounded in the knee by a fragment of a shell at Chancellorsville. Was taken prisoner on the canal near Richmond, but escaped same night. Was detailed to duty in the Confederate Arsenal where I became Assistant Superintendent of the Friction Primer Department. Was in the battles of Seven Pines, Chancellorsville, and many skirmishes. Was paroled April 14, 1865.

WILLIAM HOLMES WRIGHT

Born in Howard County, MD, Enlisted May 1861 at Leesburg, VA, as a private in Company K, First Virginia Cavalry. Afterwards in Company A, Forty-third Virginia Cavalry. Promoted sergeant in Company K. Surrendered at Paris, Fauquier County, VA, April 1865. In the battles of First Manassas, Second Manassas, Fredericksburg, Wilderness, Hanover Court House, Gettysburg, Sharpsburg, Mechanicsville, Williamsburg, and others.

JAMES HENRY WILSON

Born in Queen Anne's County, MD. Enlisted January 1862 at Heathville, VA, as a private in the Fourth Maryland Artillery. Transferred December 1864 to Company B, First Maryland Cavalry. Paroled at Richmond June 6, 1865. Wounded at Gettysburg by a shell in the knee.

WILLIAM ALEXANDER WILSON

Born in Calvert County, MD. Enlisted as a private June 1861 at Harpers Ferry in Company D, First Maryland Regiment Infantry for one year. Re-enlisted at Charlottesville September 1862 in Company B, First Maryland Cavalry for the war. Taken prisoner on retreat from Gettysburg. Remained a prisoner for 3 months. Again a captive July 29, 1864, at Chambersburg, PA. Remained a prisoner about 5 months. Participated in the following battles: First Manassas, Winchester, Gettysburg, Front Royal, and all small engagements with my command. Wounded at Clear Springs, Washington County, MD, July 29, 1864, in the right side by a Spencer Carbine ball which I carried for 20 years.

THOMAS MERRIWEATHER WALKER

Born in Richmond County, VA. Enlisted 1861 at Fort Lowry on the Rappahannock River in Company A, Fifty-sixth Virginia Infantry as a private for 3 years. Wounded in the leg at Gaines Mills. Again wounded in the hand a Petersburg. Was in the following battles: Seven Days in front of Richmond, First Fredericksburg, and all actions in which my command was engaged. On account of my wounds was detailed for guard duty at Richmond. Then sent to my home in Essex County, VA, on furlough. I was then discharged for disability.

BENJAMIN STRAWTHER WEST

Born in Fauquair County, VA. Enlisted in 1861 at Stafford County in Company A, Ninth Virginia Cavalry for the war. Was captured whilst scouting near Rapidan River. Was held one month at Old Capitol Prison in Washington, DC. Then sent to Fort Delaware for two months, then exchanged. Wounded in the shoulder at Catlett's Station, VA. Again wounded slightly below Petersburg. In the battles of Chancellorsville, Fredericksburg, Cedar Mountain, and all other actions in which my command was engaged. Paroled at Fredericksburg after the surrender of General R. E. Lee.

JOSEPH E. WATSON

Born at City of Baltimore on July 6, 1838. Enlisted spring of 1861 at Richmond in Kirby's Battery Light Artillery, Wise Legion. Term of service 4 months. Discharged at Richmond for disability. Re-enlisted summer of 1863 in Company C, Nineteenth Virginia Battalion of Heavy Artillery, Colonel Atkinson. On the day previous to General Lee's surrender sent on a fishing and forage expedition. Captured while returning by Colored Cavalry near Howard's Grove. Paroled by U.S. officer to return home and report to U.S. Provost Marshal at Richmond. Was again released on Parole with pass and transportation to Baltimore. Was taken off boat when news of Lincoln's death was received and confined in Libby Prison for a few days. Then sent to Baltimore City. Then sent to Philadelphia by of Mayor of Baltimore.

ALBERT A. WILSON
Enlisted May 18, 1861, as a private in Richmond in Company G, First Virginia Cavalry. Discharged April 1865 as a private in Richmond. Age 60 years.

HENRY FREDERICK WAGNER
Born in Baltimore September 19, 1837. Enlisted at Harpers Ferry May 13, 1861, as a private in Company D, First Maryland Infantry for one year. Re-enlisted in Breathed's Battery of Stuart's Horse Artillery in Richmond 1862. In all the engagements my two commands were in. Wounded 9th of June 1863 at Beverly's Ford. Mustered out of Service after General Lee surrendered at Appomattox Court House.

THOMAS WARD
Born in Baltimore June 15, 1843. Enlisted in the C.S. Navy for the war in the summer of 1862 at Richmond. Served on the Confederate States Steamer *Richmond*, an ironclad, until September 1864 when I was transferred to Company E, Second Maryland Infantry stationed then at Petersburg. Served in this regiment until 2 days previous to General R. E. Lee's surrender at Appomattox Court House when I was captured and carried to Libby Prison at Richmond where I remained until paroled the latter part of April same year. Was in all the battles that my two different commands were in—both on water and land. Never wounded.

SEWEL TURPIN WILLIAMS
Born at Berlin, Worcester County, MD, on January 29, 1840. Enlisted as a private for the war in Colonel Mosby's command, Forty-third Virginia Battalion in Richmond August 7, 1863. Remained with this command until close of the war. Never was captured as Mosby's men had the pick of the best horses. Never wounded. The number of engagements I was in are so numerous that it is impossible to tell them.

SWIFT AUGUSTUS WILLIAMS
Born in Caswell County, NC, October 11, 1839. Enlisted as a private in Company E, Twenty-first North Carolina Infantry for the war at Winston, NC, May 12, 1861. There I remained as a private for 12 months. Then I enlisted in the First North Carolina Battalion of Sharp Shooters where I served for the balance of the war. Entered this command also as a private, but was made sergeant. Then promoted to lieutenant. Was wounded at Rapidan Station, second Battle of Manassas. Again wounded in front of Petersburg. Never captured.

Participated in all the battles that my command was engaged in except when wounded.

WILLIAM SYDNEY WINDER

Born at Annapolis, MD, October 1, 1834. Enlisted in the year 1862 as a private in Colonel Harry Gilmor's Cavalry where I remained till detailed to act as Courier to General Bradley T. Johnson at Chambersburg, PA. With whom I remained until the close of the war. Never wounded nor a prisoner of war.

BENJAMIN YOUNG

Born in Prince George's County, MD. Enlisted February 1862 at Heathsville, VA, as a private in the Chesapeake Artillery, Fourth Maryland. Served until January 1865 at the time I was discharged at Petersburg, VA.

WILLIAM HENRY YERBY

Born at Williamsburg, VA, May 29, 1842. Enlisted at Williamsburg as a private in Company C, Thirty-second Virginia Regiment of Infantry on April 20, 1861. In which command I served till March 31, 1865, at which time I lost my left arm from a gun shot wound which laid me up for the few remaining days of the war. Was also wounded at the battle of Antietam. Never captured. Wounded and at hospital in Richmond at the time General R. E. Lee surrendered. Taken prisoner and paroled about six weeks after the fall of Richmond.

MORTIMER MILLER YOUNG

Born on the 19th of April 1825 in Richmond. Enlisted as a private in Captain Reeves' Company F, First Virginia Regiment of Infantry in Richmond in the fall of 1863. In which command I remained until the expiration of the war. Was captured at the battle of Five Forks on the 1st of April 1865. Carried to Point Lookout. Released in June 1865 after having taken the Oath of Allegiance to U.S. Government. Never wounded. Participated in all the engagements that my command was engaged in.

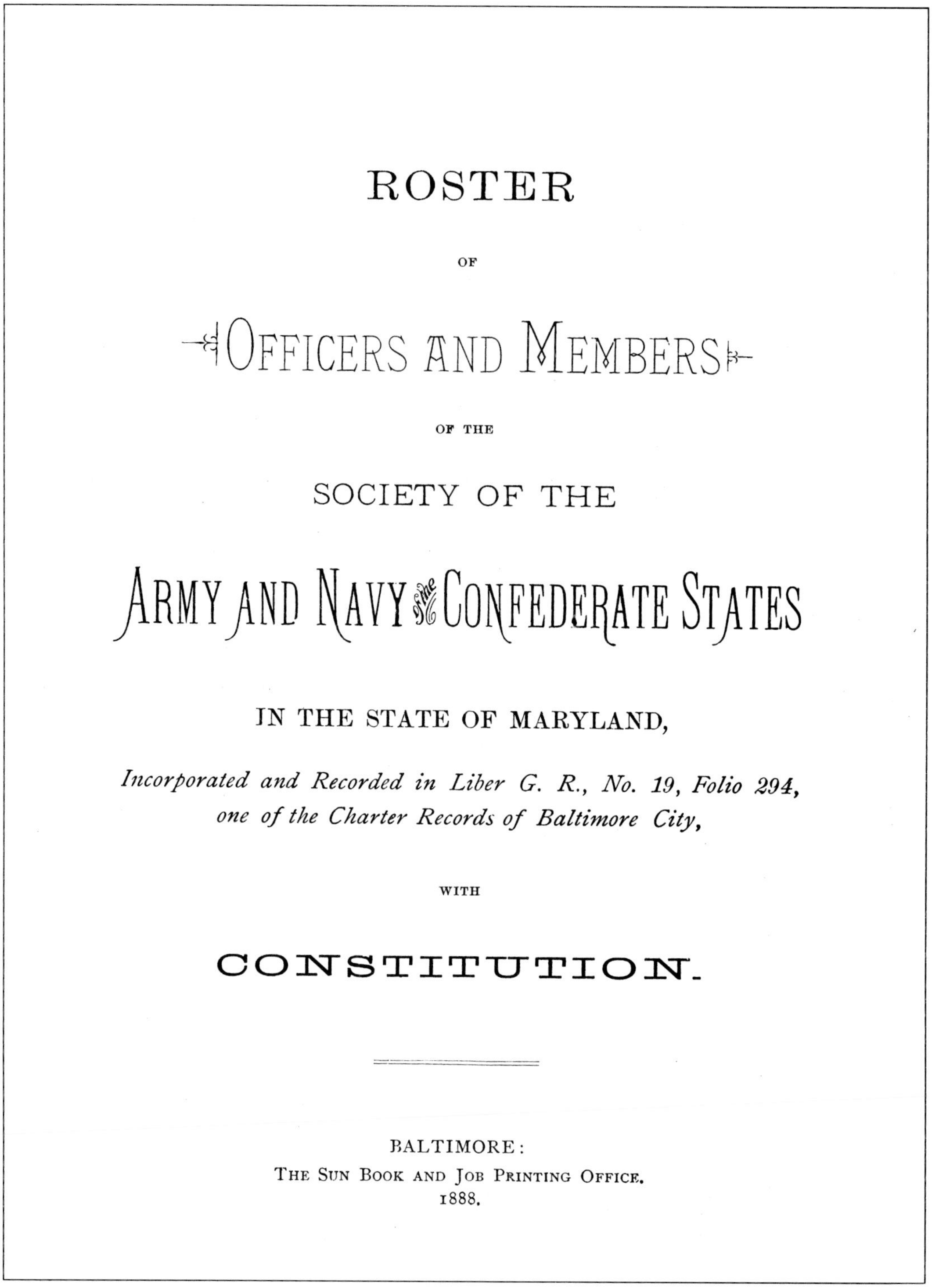

ROSTER

OF

⊰ OFFICERS AND MEMBERS ⊱

OF THE

SOCIETY OF THE

ARMY AND NAVY of the CONFEDERATE STATES

IN THE STATE OF MARYLAND,

Incorporated and Recorded in Liber G. R., No. 19, Folio 294,
one of the Charter Records of Baltimore City,

WITH

CONSTITUTION.

BALTIMORE:
THE SUN BOOK AND JOB PRINTING OFFICE.
1888.

Figure 5-1 Roster of the Society of the Army and Navy of the Confederate States in the State of Maryland, printed in 1888. (DCT)

CHAPTER FIVE

CONFEDERATE VETERANS' ORGANIZATIONS IN MARYLAND

It is somewhat surprising that a state the size of Maryland with a significant portion of its population having joined the Union war effort would have been able to support three separate and active organizations of Confederate veterans. The first of these was the Society of the Army and Navy Confederate States in the State of Maryland. Founded in 1871, it pre-dated the United Confederate Veterans by 18 years. Its stated goals were:

1. Collect and preserve material for a truthful history of the late war between the Confederate States and the United States of America.
2. Honor the memory of fallen comrades.
3. Cherish the ties of friendship among those who survived.
4. Fulfill the duties of sacred charity towards those who may stand in need of them.[1]

The Society was a statewide organization. It did not adopt a system of camps or uniform as the United Confederate Veterans did in later years. It did have an official membership badge. Section 21 of the Constitution describes it as follows:

> "The Badge of the Society shall be…the battle flag of the Confederate States, three- quarters of an inch square, in red and blue enamel, the field red, the cross blue, and the stars and border of the cross and flag of silver. In the upper quarter, 1861; in the lower quarter 1865. This square attached to the three upper arms of the

Figure 5-2 Membership badge for the Society of the Army and Navy Confederate States in the State of Maryland. Worn by Dr. Charles G. W. Macgill, Stonewall Brigade. (DCT)

Maryland Cross, which shall be of blue enamel, bordered with silver, and on it the letters A. N. C. S. Md; the whole suspended by a heavy silk ribbon, three-quarters of an inch wide, divided perpendicularly into equal red and white strips...the whole fastened with a silver clasp or buckle...."

The Society's first president was Major General Isaac R. Trimble. It had an impressive list of accomplishments by the end of its first decade of its existence.

During the war years Baltimore City was a major transfer site for Confederate POW's and the location of numerous General Hospitals. Many died from wounds or disease and needed a final resting-place. As the death toll rose during the war, residents of Baltimore who owned plots at Loudon Park Cemetery offered to trade locations with the Cemetery Company so that all the Confederates could be buried in one general area. Thus Confederate Hill was born. Shortly after the war the Loudon Park Confederate Memorial Association was formed to manage Confederate Hill and supervised the first few post-war funerals. This organization was also responsible for the erection of the monument to Confederate dead in 1870. The statue was sculpted by the famous Baltimore artist Frederick Volck. Once fully organized, the society assumed the management duties for Confederate Hill. Working with the state of Maryland, nearly $50,000 was expended on improvements and a special fund established for the permanent care of Confederate Hill by the Cemetery Company.

Another project of the Society was the return of the bodies of fallen Marylanders throughout the eastern Battlefields. Aided by an appropriation from the State Legislature, 76 Maryland Rebels were re-interred at Loudon Park Cemetery. Headstones giving each man's name, rank, and unit were placed over their graves.

In 1878 the Society donated $1,000 to the Lee Monument project in Richmond. The Society was also responsible for erecting a monument in the Maryland section of the Stonewall Jackson Cemetery at Winchester, Virginia. Dedicated in 1880, the monument was topped with a life size figure of a Maryland Infantryman.

Next came a $600.00 donation to the Southern Historical Society that was struggling to publish its history of the war in what became known as the Southern Historical Society Papers. In 1885 a very successful bazaar was held at what was then the Fifth Regiment Armory that raised over $30,000.00 for the care of Maryland veterans. Three years later this money was put to good use with the opening of the Maryland Line Confederate Soldiers' Home at Pikesville.

In 1886 the Society played a major role in the erection and dedication of the Second Maryland Infantry Monument on Culp's Hill at Gettysburg. Somewhat under-appreciated today, this was the first ever "enemy" monument on the Gettysburg Battlefield. Its final approval came not from the Parks governing body, but from the Pennsylvania Division of the Grand Army of the Republic. Every Confederate monument at Gettysburg today in some way follows the Second Maryland up the rocky slopes of Culp's Hill.

Figure 5-3 Maryland Monument at the Stonewall Jackson Cemetery in Winchester, Virginia. (DCT)

Public programs by the Society were usually limited to Confederate Memorial Day, their annual banquet, and one or two special events each year. The Society did attend the Lee Monument dedication in Richmond and the Jackson Monument in Lexington. Sometimes lectures were given and pamphlets published on a wide range of Confederate military history. By 1888 the member-

Figure 5-4 Ribbon commemorating the dedication of the Jackson Monument in Lexington, Virginia, in 1891. (DCT)

ship exceed 1,000—despite the advent of the United Confederate veterans. A roster was diligently kept of all it members and contained their name, rank, unit, and current address if still alive.[2]

The great pride that Marylanders had for their years of Confederate service showed for a second time with the formation in 1880 of the Association of the Maryland Line. The term Maryland Line is derived from the name given to regiments sent by the original 13 states to fight in the Continental Army. Maryland gained special recognition early in the war during the Battle of Long Island. The British made a surprise attack against the American left flank, causing it and the center of the line to give way. General William Alexander, commanding what was left of the right flank, realized that the American soldiers needed time to escape to Brooklyn Heights or Washington's army would be destroyed. He ordered Major Mordecai Gist to take five companies of Smallwood's Battalion, 400 men, and launch a bayonet charge directly into the path of the advancing British soldiers. At the same time General Alexander would attempt to break through the encircling British forces with the balance of his command and reach the safety of the Brooklyn defenses.

Twice Major Gist led his soon-to-be-immortal "Maryland 400" against an overwhelming number of British troops and stopped their otherwise unimpeded advance. When no more could be accomplished, Gist led the remnants of his command through the encircling enemy to the Brooklyn line. 256 men were killed or died from their wounds. Nearly every man in the battalion was wounded. As he witnessed the attack General George Washington exclaimed, "My God, what brave men I must lose today." This and other battles in the South gave the Maryland Line regiments an enviable reputation in the Continental Army.[3]

It was this proud military tradition that Bradley T. Johnson sought to replicate in the Army of Northern Virginia during the Civil War. Beginning as a major and finally Colonel of the First Maryland Infantry, he sought to combine all Maryland units under one command. Unfortunately this was not to be. The types of units in the field were not compatible to a unified command. The First Maryland Infantry had been disbanded in 1862 and replaced with the Second Battalion. Both cavalry units were only battalion strength. The First fought in the Cavalry Corps of the Army of Northern Virginia. The Second operated in the Shenandoah Valley and western Virginia. Of the four batteries of artillery, the Third spent the entire war in the Trans-Mississippi area. The First and Fourth were part of Andrew's Battalion and the Second served in the Horse Artillery.

The closest Johnson came to a unified command came during the winter of 1863-1864 when the three Eastern artillery units joined the first Cavalry and the Second Infantry in Winter Quarters at Hanover Junction, Virginia. Under Johnson's command, these units were tasked with protecting the Junction, the bridges over the North and South Anna rivers and the York River Railroad. Known as Camp St. Mary's, this was an active winter camp with numerous cavalry raids by the Army of the Potomac against Richmond. The most noteworthy being the Kilpatrick-Dalghren Raid February 28 to March 3, 1864.[4]

Ironically, what Bradley T. Johnson failed to do in time of war, may have been his greatest achievement in time of peace. Elected the first president of the Association of the Maryland Line, he directed the organization to take up two great causes. The first was to compile a roster of the eight Maryland commands in the Confederate Army and preserve the history of these fine units. The second was the creation and management of the Maryland Line Confederate Soldiers' Home at Pikesville.

With the war ended the country turned its energies to the final settlement of the Western frontier. Veterans of both armies formed strong national organizations that by 1890 wielded considerable political clout in both state and national elections. The United Confederate Veterans (UCV) was founded in 1889 to foster the activities of Southern veterans. Its counterpart was the Grand Army of the Republic (GAR). Both organizations adopted an elaborate military structure and uniform of gray or blue respectively.

The head of the United Confederate Veterans was the Commanding General with a general headquarters and staff. States were grouped into departments with each state being represented as a division. The Maryland Division included Washington, DC, and was part of the Army of Northern Virginia Department. The basic unit of organization was the "Camp" named after a leading Confederate figure either national or local. Camps were grouped into brigades. The number of brigades in a division depended on the number of camps in a state. As late as 1921 Maryland had three brigades. The First Brigade was commanded by Brigadier General Oswald Tilghman from Easton. The Second brigade was commanded by Brigadier General Frank A. Bond of Jessup. The Third Brigade was the District of Columbia under the command of Brigadier General Charles B. Howry.[5]

As mentioned earlier, Camps were grouped into brigades the same way regiments were during the war. The command structure of the Camp was highly reminiscent of a regimental staff. This tended to make these organizations top heavy in "management." As time went on the death rate left fewer active members and many of these positions went unfilled. An example of this command structure can be found in a *Sun* paper's article from January 3, 1907, announcing an election of officers for the Isaac R. Trimble Camp #1215. It must be remembered that rank given in a veteran's organization did not coincide with rank attained during the war. Thus a private could be a camp commander.

Commander – William L. Ritter
Lieutenant Commanders – Col. Winfield Peters, Wilson M. Cary,
Spottswood Bird, Charles Parkhill
Adjutant – William H. Brent
Quartermaster – M. Warner Hewes
Surgeon – Doctor John H. Grimes

Assistant Surgeons – Doctors Alexander T. Bell, J.G. Wiltshire, Louis W. Knight

Chaplains – Reverens Henry T. Sharp, William O. Maloy

Officer of the Day – George W. Walker

Paymaster – Charles Parkhill

Commissary – Edwin Kershaw

Vidette – George C. Miner

Chief Musician – Alexander J. Hubbard

Sergeant Major – Roberdean Annan

Color Guard – Sergeants Richard T. Knox and Henry Weeks

Corporals – Solomon Wright and Charles M. Jackson

Executive Committee – Gen. Andrew C. Trippe, Capt. William L. Ritter, Col. Winfield Peters, M. Warner Hewes and Charles Parkhill

Historian – Prof. Henry E. Shepherd

Figure 5-5 Confederate Veterans camp ribbon for Trimble Camp No. 1025. (D. Craig Horn)

In all there were eleven UCV Camps in Maryland. See Appendix D for a complete list of names and numbers.[6]

As a national organization the UCV sponsored annual reunions. The first was held in Chattanooga in 1899. The last was held in Norfolk, Virginia, in 1951. In its over 50 years of existence, none were ever held in Maryland. The 1917 meeting did take place in Washington DC, a part of the Maryland Division. The national office of the UCV published a magazine, "Confederate Veteran." It also published a 12-volume history of the war entitled Confederate Military History. Volume II contained the history for the state of Maryland and was written by General Bradley T. Johnson. At the state level the division commander perfected his organization while the individual camps met once a month to address local issues and arrange for patriotic events.[7]

One significant event the Maryland Division of the UCV participated in was the dedication of the Lee Monument in Richmond in 1890. Not only did the veterans attend, a large contingent of the Maryland National Guard joined forces with their counterparts in the Virginia Guard during the ceremony. After the turn of the century they would join forces again and march off to war as the famed 29th Division.

Figure 5-6 Ribbon commemorating the dedication of the Lee Monument in Richmond in 1890. Many veterans from Maryland as well as a large contingent from the Maryland National Guard attended.

Figure 5-7 The Murray Association Monument at Loudon Park Cemetery. The Association also furnished a room at the Soldiers' Home.

Besides the state and national organizations, several smaller associations also existed within the state of Maryland. The survivors of the Baltimore Light Artillery formed one such organization. Another was the Murray Association, which erected a monument on Confederate Hill at Loudon Park Cemetery. On the monument were inscribed the names of the men who served in Murray's Company H, First Maryland and Company A, Second Maryland Infantry. Both organizations furnished rooms at the Pikesville Soldiers' Home.[8]

The Sons of Confederate Veterans was officially organized at the national encampment of the United Confederate Veterans in Richmond on July 1, 1896. The original members were formed into 24 Camps. J.E.B. Stuart, Jr. was the first National Commander. Going forward their national meeting would be held each year in conjunction with that of the UCV as long as that organization had an active membership.

The head of the national organization is the Commander-in-Chief with headquarters in Hattiesburg, Mississippi. The official magazine published by the national organization is also called the "The Confederate Veteran."

The basic unit of organization is the camp that meets once a month. Camps sponsor social and educational events. A Division consists of five camps within the same state. A state convention is held once a year as well as the national meeting.

Membership requirements are that a male descendent either direct or collateral be 16 years of age and proud of his Confederate lineage.[9]

Each year the Sons of Confederate Veterans hold a ceremony at the Lee-Jackson Monument in Baltimore City on the Saturday in January nearest the two generals' birthdays. They also provide a significant presence at the annual Confederate Memorial Day ceremony at Loudon Park Cemetery. There are currently nine active camps in Maryland. See Appendix D for a complete list of active camps.

Figure 5-8 Commander's badge for the Sons of Confederate Veterans 1926 reunion in Birmingham, AL. (DCT)

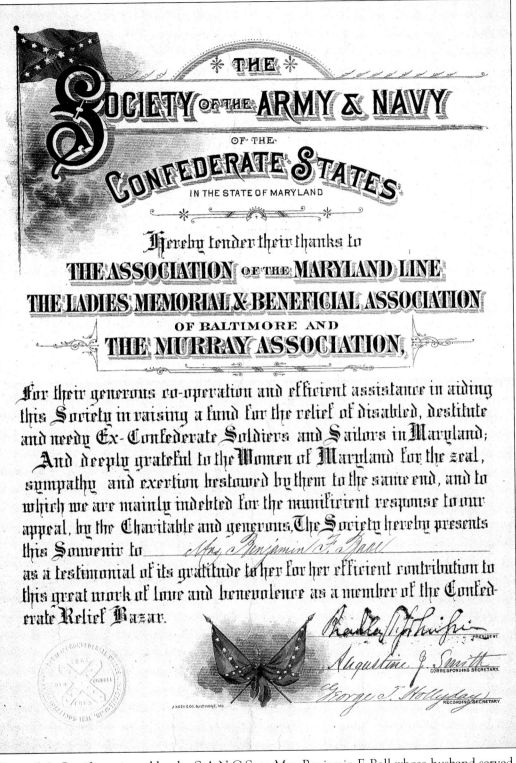

Figure 5-9 Certificate issued by the S.A.N.C.S. to Mrs. Benjamin F. Ball whose husband served in Company B, Mosby's Rangers, for her contribution to the Confederate Relief Bazaar. The document is signed by Bradley T. Johnson as president of the society and is an excellent example of the cooperation between the various post-war organizations for the good of the veterans. (DCT)

Figure 6-1 (Left) Ladies Confederate Memorial Association ribbon. Founded in 1866 this was the first post-war organization in the state to care for the veterans. (Right) Ribbon from the Ladies Committee of the Maryland Line Confederate Soldiers Home, Sept 12, 1895. (DCT)

CHAPTER SIX

UNITED DAUGHTERS OF THE CONFEDERACY

The work of Confederate women throughout the South in supporting the war effort was an often-repeated theme among the Confederate Veterans. It is not surprising that in the post-war years these same women and their descendents would work equally hard in caring for the veterans and preserving the Southern viewpoint of the War Between the States. These efforts were usually of a local nature without any state or national focus.

In Maryland the Confederate women were one jump ahead of the men who formed the Society of the Army and Navy of the Confederate States in 1871. They organized the Ladies Confederate Memorial Association of Maryland in 1866, thus being the first formal post-war organization in the state dedicated to caring for the veterans and preserving the state's Confederate heritage. As the male organizations came into existence they eagerly joined forces on such projects as the Confederate Relief Bazaar.

Needy Confederate women were not forgotten either. In 1906 the memorial Association dedicated the Confederate Women Monument at Loudon Park Cemetery with the simple inscription "To the Memory of Confederate Mothers and Widows."[1]

Through the efforts of Mrs. L.H. Rains of Savannah and Mrs. C.M. Goodlet of Nashville, a group of like-minded women met on September 10, 1894, to form a national organization that they originally called National Daughters of the Confederacy. Their objectives were to unite the numerous groups of women laboring throughout the country to care for the veterans, erect monuments, and preserve the Southern record of the war. At the second annual meeting in 1895 the word "National" was dropped from the name and it was forever known as

Figure 6-2 UDC membership pin for the Fitzhugh Lee Chapter in Frederick, MD. (DCT)

the United Daughters of the Confederacy (UDC).[2]

The seal of the organization was a reproduction of the seal of the Confederate States of America with "Daughters of the Confederacy" inscribed on the outer rim. The official badge of the UDC, after some modifications, became an enameled Confederate Flag of the Stars and Bars pattern: white, blue and scarlet in color. The flag was surrounded by a laurel wreath with the letters UDC under the flag and the numbers 61–65 on the loops of a bow tied at the bottom of the wreath.[3]

The basic unit of organization was the Chapter, usually named for a Southern personality or the city it was located in. The national organization assigned each Chapter a number in sequence with its charter. Chapters within a state formed a Division. The first Chapter formed in the Maryland Division was Baltimore #8. It was chartered on May 10, 1895.[4]

Membership in the United Daughters of the Confederacy was limited to widows, wives, mothers, sisters, and lineal descendents of men who served in the Army or Navy of the Confederate States or held a civil office in the Confederate government or one of the states comprising the Confederacy.[5]

One of the most outstanding accomplishments of the UDC was the creation and distribution of the Southern Cross of Honor. "Resolved, that the Daughters of the Confederacy, do confer upon each and every member of the Army and Navy of the Confederate States of America, a cross…to be handed down from one generation to another as a most priceless heritage…"

The final design of the cross was approved at the 1899 convention in Richmond. It called for a bronze cross with a battle flag on its face, surrounded by a wreath of laurel. On the obverse is printed the inscription "United Daughters Confederacy to the U.C.V." On the reverse is the inscription "Southern Cross of Honor" and within the wreath "Deo Vindice" (God and Vindicator). The cross was suspended from a pin bar that allowed the name of the recipient to be inscribed on the bar.

A patent for the medal was secured on February 20, 1900, and the first order of 2,500 crosses completed on April 17. So popular

Figure 6-3 Southern Cross of Honor awarded to Payton R. Harrison. (DCT)

was this device that 12,500 were issued during the first 18 months of its existence. Between 1907 and 1913, 78,761 Southern Crosses of Honor were issued.[6]

During a ceremony held in 1908 at the Pikesville Soldiers' Home to commemorate the centennial birthday of Jefferson Davis, the Maryland Division of the UDC presented nine Crosses of Honor to the following veterans:

Francis E. Bond – Baltimore	J. T. Fenal – Pikesville
John F. Duke – Leonardtown	James Price – Pikesville
Harris Hough – Rolland Oak	J. C. Snowden – Pikesville
Jullan M. Spencer – Annapolis	William H. Yerby – Pikesville
Thomas C. Stringer – Baltimore	

As a result of World War I, the UDC created a medal for direct descendents of Confederate soldiers who served in the American Expeditionary Force. The medal, to be known as the Cross of Military Service, was approved at the 1922 convention in Birmingham. The design consisted of a cross the same shape and size as the Cross of Honor with a Crusaders Cross affixed to its center with a Confederate Battle Flag. On the obverse are the dates 1917–1918 and the Latin phrase "Fortes creantur fortibus" (The brave give birth to the brave). The device is connected to a red, white, red ribbon with an entwined monogram UDC. Slightly altered versions of the Cross of Military Service were also issued for World War II and the Korean War.

On April 21, 1954, the William H. Murray Chapter hosted the semi-annual convention of the Maryland Division of the UDC at Christ Church at West River, Anne Arundel County. Dr. Brice M. Dorsey received a Cross of Military Service for his service in World War II. Mr. William S. Clark also received a Cross for serving during the Korean War.[7]

In 1960 the Maryland Division of the UDC consisted of 10 camps. By the year 2000 there were still 8 active chapters in the state. Over the past century the ladies of the UDC have taken on many challenges and accomplished much in the preservation of Maryland's Confederate heritage. In 1903 the Maryland UDC erected the Confederate Soldiers and Sailors Monument at Mount Royal Avenue and Mosher Street.[8]

Members of the UDC were the driving force in the erection of the Confederate

Figure 6-4 Cross of Military Service awarded to Henry McP. Longue Jr. for his service in WWI by the William H. Murray Chapter in Annapolis, MD. Henry McP. Longue served as a Corporal in Co. B 39th Virginia Cavalry. (Jack Kelbaugh)

Women's Monument in 1918 at University Parkway and Charles Street. Representatives from the UDC petitioned both houses of the State Legislature for funds, that together with private donations eventually led to the completion of the monument.[9]

Covered in Chapter Three were the many years of dedicated service the ladies gave the veterans living at the Pikesville Soldiers' Home. With the declining population at the home, the ladies of the UDC arranged for many of the finest artifacts from the Relic Hall to be transferred to the Maryland Historical Society in 1920. A special room was established in 1937 known as "The Confederate Room." Furnished with matching display cases of walnut and glass, the room was filled with uniforms, weapons, photographs, and flags of the Confederacy. The room was closed in 1988. It reopened in November of 1991 as a combined exhibit of the Society's Union and Confederate relics. The exhibit is now known as "Maryland in the Civil War, A House Divided."[10]

In 1946 Mrs. Guy Hudson Parr, President of the Maryland Division of the UDC, appointed Mrs. James McClure Gillet Chairman of the Restoration Committee for Loudon Park's revered old Confederate Hill. On a visit to Confederate Hill Mrs. Parr found that many of the stones had fallen over and the entire area was in need of repairs of one kind or another. Told no funding

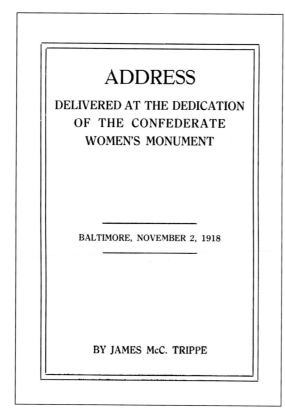

Figure 6-5 (L) Address delivered by James Trippe at the dedication of the Women's Monument. (R) Early postcard view of the Confederate Women's Monument. (DCT)

was available she determined to restore the Hill if she had to do the work one grave at a time. The cemetery company agreed to do the repair work at cost. By 1950, 132 graves had been restored. Two years later one third of the 700 gravesites had been refurbished. Markers were secured for the last two veterans buried from the Pikesville home and one for General Thomas G. Rhett.

In the course of the restoration project every effort was made to preserve the identities of the deceased soldiers. The names of all that could be identified were arranged by state and an article describing the restoration project published in the UDC magazine.[11]

It is truly remarkable how the women of the UDC perceived their goals and the means to accomplish them. Realizing that no organization's membership is permanent, the ladies of the UDC looked at their children as the next generation of SCV and UDC. To this end Mrs. E.G. McCabe of Atlanta proposed at the national convention in Baltimore in 1897 that each chapter of the UDC have a children's chapter within its organization. The new organization would be known as the Mary Custis Lee Children of the Confederacy.

The objective of this organization is to involve the children of the South in some work to aid and honor Confederate veterans and their descendents. Each chapter could take a local name and was under a Directress. The seal of this organization is the battle flag and last official flag of the Confederacy crossed and surmounted by a wreath of laurel. On the outer rim is engraved "Mary Custis Lee Children of the Confederacy."

The membership badge is a simple piece of white ribbon with Mary Custis Lee Children of the Confederacy stamped in red ink on it. The maximum age for membership is 17. At age 18 the members can join the UDC or the SCV.[12]

An example of activities participated in by Children of the Confederacy was seen in 1952 when the Samuel Sutherland Chapter COC placed flowers on the graves at Loudon Park for the annual Confederate Memorial Day ceremony.[13]

Figure 7-1 Confederate Women's Home. (DCT)

CHAPTER SEVEN

THE CONFEDERATE WOMEN'S HOME

The story of the Maryland Line Confederate Soldiers' Home at Pikesville is well documented in this book. A much less known story is that of the Confederate Women's Home. This home was maintained for many years through the singular generosity of one man, Mr. James R. Wheeler. A veteran of the First Maryland Cavalry, James Wheeler returned to Baltimore City after the war and was successful in a number of business ventures. He was also the president of the Commonwealth Bank of Baltimore.

The first home for Confederate women was opened on Mulberry Street in 1885. It was later moved to a site on Charles Street and finally to the Baker Mansion on Fulton Avenue. When a lack of funds threatened to close the home, Mr. Wheeler offered the use of his townhouse at 1020 Linden Avenue rent-free.[1]

The Confederate Women's Home opened on September 1, 1906. Mr. Wheeler was the President, Treasurer, and chief benefactor. He was aided in this endeavor by a group of 10 vice-presidents and 10 managers. Additional money for the Home came from fundraising events and a payment of $50.00 per month from the state of Maryland.[2]

Mr. Wheeler also realized that many of the women at the home would need a final resting-place. He acquired several burial lots near Confederate Hill in Loudon Park Cemetery. On October 15, 1913, the Board of Managers from the Home dedicated a monument for all the women who would be interred there. The granite marker bears a simple inscription, "Confederate Women" on the front and a bronze plaque on the reverse side.[3]

There are a total of ten women buried from the Home at Loudon Park. Their area is maintained today by the James R. Wheeler Chapter #1859 of the UDC. The chapter was chartered in 1924 and named for this great man.[4]

Figure 7-2 Confederate Women's Monument at Loudon Park Cemetery showing bronze plaque on the reverse side. (Donna Williams)

The Home on Linden Avenue opened with six women in residence. During its first six years it sheltered a total of 21 women. Seven of these died during the same time period. By 1925, a total of 28 women had lived there.[5]

After 16 years of faithful service to the women of the Confederacy, Mr. Wheeler died on January 24, 1924. In his will the property on Linden Avenue went to his heirs. He did leave the sum of $1,000.00 to the Home to help meet its future needs.

The Board of Directors, now expanded to 12, determined to manage the Home. Each Director obligated themselves to managing the Home one month out of the year.[6]

In September of 1925, the six remaining residents at the Home were transferred to a new location. This was at 6000 Bellona Avenue in Govans. The women by this time ranged in age from 80 to 86.[7]

Figure 7-3 Souvenir program for benefit performance held at Albaugh's Theatre in 1913 to aid the Confederate Women's Home. (DCT)

Figure 8-1 Silk commemorative ribbon for Confederate
Memorial Day. (DCT)

CHAPTER EIGHT

CONFEDERATE MEMORIAL DAY

No event illustrates the passion, dedication and pride Marylanders have for their Confederate heritage more than the annual Confederate Memorial Day ceremony at Loudon Park Cemetery. The Society of the Army and Navy of the Confederate States in Maryland began making arrangements for this event in 1873.[1]

This ceremony has always been a collaboration between the veterans when they were alive and the ladies of the UDC. An example of a peak year for this program was 1881. The executive committee of the Society of the Army and Navy of the Confederate States in Maryland consisted of General Bradley T. Johnson, Colonel J. Lyle Clark, Sergeant William H. Pope, Mr. Ridgley Brown and H. H. Garrigues.

Beginning at 1 PM the Catonsville Railroad ran cars every half-hour. At 3:30 a train of 7 cars left Calvert Street Station. A second train of 7 cars followed 10 minutes later. The two combined to carry 600 persons. As visitors arrived they left the coaches and passed among the graves placing flowers on each and every one of them. At 4:15 the procession formed at the Frederick Road entrance. General George H. Steuart, Vice President of the Society, was the Grand Marshal. At the head of the procession was a contingent of 15 Baltimore City policemen. They were followed by the Charles Monument Band. Then came 140 members of the Society of the Army and Navy of the Confederate States in Maryland led by their president, Lt. McHenry Howard. This group was followed by literally hundreds of men, women and children. Among those on the reviewing stand were General Johnson, General James R. Herbert, General Isaac R. Trimble, and the historian J. Thomas Scharf. A prayer was given by Rev. William M. Dame. Captain J. Hampden Chamberlayne delivered the oration of the day.[2]

By 1910 the number of veterans attending the Memorial Day ceremony was greatly diminished, but not their sense of duty to be there. Sixty-eight veterans from the Pikesville Home attended under the command of Captain R .J. Stinson. The official procession formed at 4:00 PM. It was led by the Feidmann's City Park Band. Rev. William M. Dame opened the ceremonies with a prayer. Then his son, Rev. William Page Dame delivered the main address.[3]

The governors of the Maryland Line Confederate Soldiers' Home at Pikesville meet on December 9, 1928. At an average age of 86 years, these old veterans were wisely feeling the need to cut back on their activities. They determined that it was time to turn the Memorial Day event over to the United Daughters of the Confederacy.[4]

The 1928 ceremony was attended by an ever-shrinking number of veterans from the Pikesville Home and a handful of Confederate widows. Twelve veterans were present. Three were so feeble that they remained in the cars that brought them. Three members of the Pikesville board of directors were also in attendance. R. T. Richardson 88, E. S. Dance 85, and Mr. Tunis, superintendent of the Home, was 86 years of age.

One widow from the Confederate Women's Home was also there, Mrs. Rebecca Dorsey. The two other surviving residents were too feeble to attend. Mrs. R. W. MacCubbin whose husband was a member of the Baltimore Light Artillery was also in attendance.

The ceremony was held for the first time under the auspices of the Maryland Division of the United Daughters of the Confederacy. The program was arranged by the James R. Wheeler Chapter.[5]

To this day Confederate Memorial Day is a well-attended event. Members of the Sons of Confederate Veterans have replaced the original veterans and a new generation of ladies from the United Daughters of the Confederacy attend to the many details that makes this event a landmark in Maryland Civil War heritage.

Figure 8-2 The author delivers the keynote address during the 125th annual ceremony on Confederate Hill to celebrate Confederate Memorial Day. (Elliott Cummings)

CONFEDERATE MEMORIAL DAY.

JUNE 6TH, 1902.

ORDER OF EXERCISES AT LOUDON PARK.

Procession will form at Main Entrance at 4 o'clock
and march to Confederate Lot.

Music by the Fifth Regiment Veteran Corps Band,
W. H. PINDELL, Leader.

PRAYER............................*Rev. Wm. M. Dame.*

"HOW SLEEP THE BRAVE"...................*Male Chorus.*

ADDRESS.....................*Captain Henry E. Shepherd.*

"BLESSED ARE THEY".....................*Male Chorus.*

"THE CONQUERED BANNER".........*Miss Katie McWilliams.*

HYMN ("*Just As I Am*").....................*Male Chorus.*

BENEDICTION.

HYMN ("*Nearer, My God, to Thee*")......*Audience, With Band.*

Before the exercises, flowers will be strewn by the Daughters
of the Confederacy and other ladies.

(OVER.)

Figure 8-3 Program for the 1902 Confederate Memorial Day. (DCT)

BOARD OF GOVERNORS AND MANAGERS.

No. 1. JAS. R. WHEELER, *Chairman*.   No. 5. AUGUST SIMON,
"   2. COL. GEO. R. GAITHER,   "   6. CHAS. KETTLEWELL,
"   3. R. J. STINSON,   "   7. DAN'L L. THOMAS,
"   4. MARK O. SHRIVER,   "   8. CAPT. CHAS. H. CLAIBORNE.

APPENDIX A

ASSOCIATION OF THE MARYLAND LINE
President
General Bradley T. Johnson
Secretary: Captain George W. Booth   Corresponding Secretary: John F. Hayden
Treasure: William H. Fitzgerald

BOARD OF GOVERNORS

James R. Wheeler	R. J. Stinson	A. C. Trippe	Mark O. Shriver
August Simon	John W. Torsch	Charles Kettlewell	Charles H. Claiborne
Daniel L. Thomas	James L. Aubrey	George R. Gaither	John F. Hayden

MANAGERS CONFEDERATE SOLDIERS' HOME
James R. Wheeler, Chairman
August Simon
George R. Gaither
Bradley T. Johnson, ex-officio
George W. Booth, ex-officio
William H. Fitzgerald, ex-officio

BOARD OF VISITORS
President: Mrs. Bradley T. Johnson, Vice-President: Mrs. William H. Brune
Corresponding Secretary: Mrs. Carey B. Gamble
Recording Secretary: Mrs. D.G. Wright

EXECUTIVE COMMITTEE
Mrs. W. P. Zollinger   Mrs. Charles Harrison   Mrs. John P. Poe.

GENERAL MEMBERSHIP BOARD OF VISITORS
Mrs. Fielder C. Slingluff, W.R. McKnew, L. McLane Tiffany, A. Hawksley, L.N. Hopkins, High S. Lee, D.G. McIntosh, Edwin Warfield, Samuel J. Hough, W.C.Nicholas, L.H. Tegmeyer, W.H. Marriott, Harvey Jones, J.F.C. Talbott, M.H. Thomas, R.P.H. Staub, W.B. Wilson, John Gill, M.B. Brown, B.F. Smith, Harry F. Turner, A.T. Parron, George W. Lay, B.H. Richards, Richard Morton, Philip, W.T. Thelin, Frank Markoe, W.P. Zollinger, B.H. Ramsay, G.T.M.

Gibson, E.B. Powell, F. Miles, Carey B. Gamble, T.F. Meyer, R. Millikin, Eugene VanNess, Neilson Poe, Wardlaw, J.C. Wrenshall, Alfred Powell, John P. Poe, Isaac Nicholson, Fred Smith, J.R. Herbert, Bradley T. Johnson, Wilcox Brown, A.J. Gosman, D.D. Giraud Wright, Hunter Johnson, C.L. Rogers, W.H. Blackford, John Brosius, H.A. Ramsay, Eugene Blackford, J.J. Boykin, W.G. Power, Thomas Craddock, W.B. Davidson, W.H. Brune, Clarence Cottman, I.E. Emerson, R.B. Winder, Joseph Brinkley, R.R. Buck, J.L. Bent, Frank P. Clark, W.R. Dorsey, W.B. Graves, H.F. Going, C.R. Goodwin.

Miss Julia McHenry, Dora Hoffman, E. McCandlish, Maud Whiting, E.B. Smyrk, Mordecai, E. Andrews, King, K. Anderson, Duval.

APPENDIX B

INVENTORY OF THE RELIC HALL

O ver the years at least three different lists were published describing items loaned or given to the Soldiers' Home that were on display in the Relic Hall or throughout the buildings within the old walled complex. Some lists grouped the items by the donor or gave a brief history of the item. Others simply stated "#111 Confederate Battle Flag." The author has carefully compared these lists in an attempt to eliminate duplications and grouped items belonging to a particular individual together to make their existence more meaningful. A perfect accounting of this collection is impossible, as many relics that would be highly sought after personal items today did not warrant a great deal of attention 100 years ago. Thus a spoon was only a spoon even if it did belong to a private in the First Maryland Cavalry. Here then is what was likely to have been seen in the rooms, corridors, and the Relic Hall of the Maryland Line Confederate Soldiers' Home.

LOANED BY GENERAL BRADLEY T. JOHNSON

1. The Stars and Bars (first Confederate flag) presented to Captain E. R. Dorsey's Co. C, 1st Maryland Regiment at Richmond in May, 1861.

2. State Flag sent from Baltimore to 1st MD Regiment at Fairfax, VA, in August 1861, and used on parade occasions and also on the bier of Gen. Charles Sidney Winder.

3. Battle Flag of the 1st MD Regiment with "Bucktail." This flag was brought by Miss Hetty Cary from Baltimore to Virginia through the blockade and presented to the regiment on its arrival at Manassas Junction on the morning of July 21, 1861. It was carried through 1st Manassas and in every skirmish and action of the Army in 1861, through Jackson's Valley Campaign, where it was borne with the advance guard

on the advance and the rear guard on the retreat and through Seven Days Battles. It was carried near Ashby when he was killed in the battle at Harrisonburg June 6, 1862, and decorated by General Order No. 30, June 12, 1862: the 1st MD Regiment was ordered to affix a Bucktail to its colors in honor of its gallantry in avenging the death of Ashby. The identical Bucktail is now appended to the colors. On disbanding of the regiment the colors were presented to Mrs. Bradley T. Johnson.

4. Letter from Edwin Selvage, Color Bearer, and the First Sergeants of the 1st MD Regiment, presenting the Bucktail Flag to Mrs. Johnson.
5. Bunting Flag with Maryland State Arms.
6. Cocked Hat Note. Official form in which paroles and counter-signs were sent to Colonel Elzey, 4th Brigade, at Winchester, June and July 1861.
7. Miniature Flag presented by Gen. Beauregard to Mrs. Johnson about June 1, 1861.
8. An original Act of the Confederate Congress, signed by Jefferson Davis, President, A.H. Stephens, Vice-President, and Thomas S. Bocock, Speaker of the House.
9. Spur of Col. Harry Gilmor.
10. Resolutions of the officers of the 1st MD Regiment, thanking Mrs. Johnson for her services in equipping the Maryland Line, passed at Harpers Ferry in 1861.
11. Saddle-Girth exchanged by Col. A. P. Hill, 13th VA Regiment, with Col. Johnson 1st MD, for a Chaplain.
12. A Match Box taken from the haversack of a dead soldier in Burnside's Battery at Henry House, Manassas, July 21, 1861.
13. Original Muster Roll of Company B, 21st VA Regiment, Captain James Lyle Clarke, a Maryland Company.
14. Commission of Bradley T. Johnson, Col. 1st MD Regiment which was accompanied by an order to organize all Marylanders in the Army of Northern Virginia into the Maryland Line, which was placed under his command in October, 1863.
15. Photograph of President Davis with an autographed letter.
16. Photograph of Lt. Gen. A. P. Hill.
17. Photograph of Maj. Gen. Arnold Elzey.
18. Maryland Cockade, Baltimore, April 19, 1861.
19. Breastplate taken from a Major in the 1st New York Cavalry at the battle of Winchester in May of 1862.
20. Carbine taken at Harpers Ferry.
21. Sergeant's Sword, 6th Mass. Regiment taken by Marshal Kane April 19, 1861, and given to then Captain B. T. Johnson of the Maryland Milita.
22. Sergeant's Sword captured in battle.
23. Two Sword Bayonets from 2nd Manassas.
24. Sash and Sword captured at Winchester in May of 1862.
25. Souvenir Shield, containing a saber presented by Gen. Wade Hampton

to Colonel Johnson in recognition of services in saving Richmond from Kilpatrick and Dahlgren.

26. Saber with steel scabbard imported from Bermuda through the blockade in Dec. 1861.

27. Sword given to B.T. Johnson by Mrs. Johnson.

28. Sword from Thomas H. Wynne, President Richmond City Council to Col. Johnson.

29. War sash.

30. Portrait of Stonewall Jackson by Elder.

31. Portrait of Gen. Jubal A. Early.

32. Coat in which Gen. Turner Ashby was killed June 6, 1862.

33. Pike taken from John Brown at Harpers Ferry, October 1859.

34. General Order No. 30, June 12, 1862, Headquarters Ewell's Division, complimenting 1st MD Regiment for avenging the death of Ashby.

35. Battle Flag Maryland Colors. Presented to the Frederick Volunteers May 1861 and carried by Co. A, 1st MD Regiment up to and including 1st Manassas, July 21, 1861.

36. Headquarters Guidon of Johnson's Cavalry Brigade, A.N.V., June to December 1864.

37. Battle Flag First Maryland Cavalry, which they refused to surrender at Appomattox. Sgt. Dorsey, Co. A, tore the flag from the staff, concealed it on his body, and carried it to Bedford County, VA, where he deposited it with a young lady for safe-keeping. She has restored it to the Association of the Maryland Line.

38. Special Order, complimenting 1st MD Regiment June 22, 1861.

39. Original Invoice of Arms and Equipment, for 500 men issued by the State of North Carolina to Mrs. Bradley T. Johnson May 28, 1861.

40. Order from General Beauregard to delay the train for Mrs. Johnson and the arms.

41. Receipt to Mrs. Johnson from G. M. Cochran, Master of Ordinance, Harpers Ferry for 500 muskets dated June 3, 1861.

42. Requisition from Captain William W. Goldsborough, Co. A, 1st MD Regiment for clothing dated August 10, 1861.

43. Uniform of a Confederate Brigadier General.

44. Uniform of Sgt. William H. Pope Co. A, 1st MD Cavalry. Jacket, paints, hat, saber, pistol and holster, two ambrotypes and a letter brought from the Seven Days Battlefield around Richmond.

45. Account of Expenses for Headquarters Staff Maryland Line, January 1864.

46. Topography Map of the Shenandoah Valley issued by Engineer Corps to commanders of brigades, July to November 1864.

47. Last Order of Maj. Gen. J.E.B. Stuart, 9 a.m. May 11, 1864.

48. Johnson's commission as colonel of the 1st MD Regiment.

49. Returns of Election, February 10, 1864, for colonel of the Maryland Line.

50. Original copy of "My Maryland."
51. General Order No. 75 A.N.V., July 7, 1862, Headquarters in the field.
52. General Order No. 65, October 31, 1863, Ewell's Corps, complimenting the 1st MD Battalion of Infantry on its being assigned to the Maryland Line.
53. General Order Stuart's Brigade, November 1, 1863, complimentary.
54. Special Order No. 1, April 26, 1865. Adjutant's and Inspector General's office C.S., Charlotte, NC, granting honorable discharge to all Marylanders. The last order issued by Maj. Gen. John C. Breckenridge, Secretary of War, CSA.
55. Enfield Musket from C.S. ironclad *City of Richmond*.
56. Muster Rolls of Maryland Line.

LOANED BY THE RICHMOND CLUB
57. Portrait of General Robert E. Lee.

LOANED BY GENERAL CUSTIS LEE
58. Sword of General Robert E. Lee.
59. One pair gauntlets of General Robert E. Lee.
60. One large French telescope of General Robert E. Lee.
61. One Texas saddle of General Robert E. Lee.

LOANED BY MRS. GEN. J. E. B. STUART
62. Portrait of Major General J.E.B. Stuart.
63. Hat worn by General Stuart.
64. One pair gauntlets worn by General Stuart.
65. Sash of General Stuart.
66. One pair gold spurs of General Stuart.
67. Prayer book carried by General Stuart during the war.
68. Candle and candlestick of General Stuart.
69. Order assigning Stuart to Harpers Ferry as a Lt. Colonel.
70. Stuart's commission as Lt. Colonel.
71. Stuart's commission as Brigadier General.
72. Stuart's commission as Major General.
73. Autographed letter from General Joseph H. Johnson to General Stuart.
74. Autographed letter from General R. E. Lee to General Stuart.

LOANED BY GENERAL JOSEPH JOHNSTON
75. Headquarters Flag of General Joseph E. Johnston.

LOANED BY GENERAL P.G.T. BEAUREGARD
76. Headquarters flag of General Beauregard.
77. Headquarters flag of General Earl Van Dorn.
   (These three flags were the pattern of the Confederate Battle Flag. They

were made by the three Cary sisters of Baltimore and presented to the above named generals.

78. General Stonewall Jackson's camp stool.

LOANED BY GENERAL WADE HAMPTON

79. Sword of Col. Wade Hampton worn at the battle of Eutaw, June 7, 1782, and by his grandson Col. Wade Hampton, at the First Battle of Manassas, July 21, 1861.

LOANED BY THE SOUTHERN HISTORICAL SOCIETY

80. Original Constitution of the Confederate States.
81. Great Seal of the Confederate States.
82. President Davis' letter to General Joseph E. Johnston, April 24, 1865, approving of the convention with General Sherman.

LOANED BY LUTHER ASHBY

83. Flag of General Turner Ashby.

LOANED BY CAPTAIN JAMES I. WADDELL

84. Original order to command the CSS *Shenandoah*.
85. Log book of the CSS *Shenandoah*.
86. Chart showing the track of the ship around the world.
87. One pair of brass dividers.
88. Sword of Captain Waddell.
89. Battle Flag of the CSS *Shenandoah*.
90. Flag adopted by the Confederate Congress in 1864 on a brass tripod and picture of Captain Waddell attached to it representing when he took command of the ship.
91. Oil painting of the C.S.S. *Shenandoah* by De Boen.
92. Small items of ivory made by crewmembers of the *Shenandoah*.
93. Last Navy Register issued by the Confederate Navy Department.

LOANED BY MRS. ADMIRAL BUCHANAN

94. Picture of the C. S. Ironclad *Virginia*.
95. Uniform coat worn by Admiral Franklin Buchanan in the engagement between the *Virginia* and the *Monitor* at Hampton Roads.
96. Uniform overcoat of Admiral Franklin Buchanan.

LOANED BY RIDGELY BROWN

97. Appomattox Parole of a private in the Second Maryland Infantry, April 9, 1865.
98. Photograph and bullets from the battle of Gettysburg.
99. Descriptive List of a soldier dated February 24, 1865.

LOANED BY LT. JAMES W. DAVIS

100.   Sole remains of regimental flag of the 26th Virginia Regiment, which was used in the Battle of the Crater July 30, 1864. After the battle Lt. Davis found the staff with only a small piece of the flag still attached.

101.   Small brick made of clay from the crater.

LOANED BY THE STONEWALL BRIGADE BAND

102.   The instruments used by the Stonewall Brigade Band during the war and at the surrender at Appomattox were brought home by the members who were by order of General Grant allowed to retain them.

LOANED BY MOZART HAYDEN

103.   Nearly complete collection of Confederate Treasury notes.

LOANED BY COL. EDWARD McCRADY OF SC

104.   The flag presented to Gregg's 1st South Carolina Volunteers after the battle of Fort Sumter and on the departure of the regiment for Virginia April 22, 1861. At the battle of Cold Harbor June 27, 1862, all the Color Guards (Taylor, Hayne, Pinkney, and Gregg) were killed or wounded around it, Taylor's blood being still on the flag.

105.   Battle Flag of the 10th South Carolina Volunteers, Gen. Manigault's regiment.

106.   The last flag that floated from Fort Sumter and which was taken down on its evacuation by Confederate troops.

107.   Flag of the Washington Light Infantry.

LOANED BY W. S. POWELL

108.   Collection of C. S. Treasury notes.

109.   Last draft drawn by the C. S. Treasurer for interest on public debt.

LOANED BY MRS. WILLIAM ALLAN

110.   Letter from General R. E. Lee to Mr. Samuel H. Tagart, Esq., supposed to be the last he ever wrote.

111.   Brass eagle made from a piece of the CSS *Virginia*.

LOANED BY MRS. GENERAL EDWIN LEE

112.   Photographs of General R. E. Lee's body lying in state and of the obsequies.

113.   John Brown's spy glass taken by then Lt. Edwin Lee from his cabin on Maryland Heights October 1859.

114.   General Pendleton's Letter and Order Book.

LOANED BY CAPT. E. T. JACKSON

115.   Regimental Battle Flag of the 22nd Virginia Infantry, torn with shot and

shell and stained with blood. The day Lee surrendered at Appomattox, Capt. Jackson was the senior regimental officer and marched away with a dozen men taking the colors and never surrendering.

LOANED BY COL. WILLIAM NORRIS

116. Signal flag.
117. Confederate flag from the tug *Torpedo* in the battle of Hampton Roads.
118. Confederate flag, third issue.
119. General Beauregard's battle flag.
120. Boat pennant from the *Merrimac*.
121. Signal Corps spy glass.
122. Lantern for making night signals.

LOANED BY MRS. COL. D. G. McINTOSH

123. Battle Flag of Pegram's Artillery Battalion, A. P. Hill's Corps. Carried in the battles of 1st Manassas, Sevens Days, Cedar Mountain, 2nd Manassas, Chantilly, Harpers Ferry, Sharpsburg, Fredericksburg, Chancellorsville, Gettysburg, Wilderness, Spottsylvania, North Anna, Cold Harbor, The Crater, Hatcher's Run, Appomattox.
124. Battle Flag of McIntosh's Artillery Battalion. Presented by Captain McIntosh to his battery in 1862 and borne by his battalion to Appomattox.

LOANED BY DR. CHARLES PERCIVAL

125. Sword from the battle of Sharpsburg inscribed "Captain C. C. Knowles, First Regiment Alabama Volunteers."

LOANED BY CAPTAIN J. W. CLARK, AUGUSTA, GA

126. Flag of Cobb's Legion.
127. Flag of Seventh Georgia Cavalry.
128. Headquarters Flag of Cobb's Brigade.
129. Flag of the gunboat *Teaser* in the battle of Hampton Roads.
130. Flag of Stamford's Mississippi Battery, Army of Tennessee.

LOANED BY GENERAL ISAAC R. TRIMBLE

131. Five orders (framed) issued by Gen. Trimble in Baltimore April and May 1861.

LOANED BY CAPTAIN J. W. TORSCH

132. Official copy of the military convention between generals Grant and Lee, April 9, 1865, and a copy of General Lee's farewell order to the Army of Northern Virginia—General Order No. 9.
133. Muster Roll of the Second Maryland Infantry surrendered at Appomattox.

134. Grant's letter to Lee April 10, 1865.
135. Flowers presented by General R. E. Lee to Miss Wallis on the morning of the battle of Sharpsburg.
136. Flag of the Second South Carolina Volunteers.

LOANED BY MRS. CHARLES F. BONAPARTE

137. Miniature of Jerome Bonaparte
138. Gun presented to Jerome Napoleon Bonaparte by his father.
139. Pistols presented to Jerome Bonaparte by the Duke of Brunswick.
140. Money box belonging to Elizabeth Patterson Bonaparte.

LOANED BY MISS BAKER, AUGUSTA, GA

141. Flag of the Fourth Battalion Georgia Sharpshooters.

LOANED BY J. N. CRAIG, ESQ.

142. Book found on the body of Captain E. J. Harris, 49th North Carolina Infantry. Stained with his blood at the battle of the Crater, July 30, 1864.

LOANED BY MISS IDA MASON

143. Commission of James M. Mason, Envoy Extraordinary and Minister Plenipotentiary to the Queen of Great Britain.

LOANED BY COL. CHARLES MARSHALL

144. General Lee's headquarters camp table.
145. Gun made from brass of the Virginia.

LOANED BY MISS DORA HOFFMAN

146. Lock of President Davis' hair.

LOANED BY MISS FLORENCE MACKUBIN

147. Photograph of Jefferson Davis and C. C. Clay just after they were released from Fortress Monroe.
148. Wreath from the coffin of Jefferson Davis.
149. Pistol carried by President Davis throughout the war in his breast pocket. Captain John Taylor Wood picked it up at the door of the tent as he and General Breckenridge escaped after the capture of Mr. Davis.

LOANED BY MISS MANLY

150. Autographed letter from President Davis to Miss Manly of Newbern, NC.

LOANED BY MISS KING

151. Engraving of President Davis when he was the U.S. Secretary of War.

LOANED BY MRS. FITZHUGH LEE

152. General R. E. Lee's Spurs.
153. General R. E. Lee's Saddle, Bridle and Bit—the equipment of Traveler.
154. General R. E. Lee's Headquarter Battle Flag.

LOANED BY MRS. GEORGE R. GOLDSBOROUGH

155. General Lee's camp coffee pot.

LOANED BY MRS. BEVERLEY R. CODWISE

156. A hat given to Gen. Lee by the lady who made it and by him given to a soldier.

LOANED BY MRS. CHARLES MARSHALL

157. Original order signed by General Lee.

LOANED BY MRS. MARIAN C. GAMBRILL

158. Sword of General Lee presented by him to Captain Chapman Maupin.
159. Copy of Lee's Farewell to the Army of Northern Virginia.

LOANED BY MRS. ROBERT ATKINSON

160. General Lee's prayer book given to him by Bishop Atkinson.

LOANED BY MISS K. M. ROWLAND

161. Lock of General Lee's hair.

LOANED BY CAPTAIN JOHN D. SMITH

162. Autographed picture of General Lee on Traveler.

LOANED BY DR. PRESTON

163. Small bust of General Lee by Ezekiel.

LOANED BY SAMUEL K. GEORGE, ESQ.

164. Autographed picture of General Lee and the hat cord worn by him during the war. All presented to his cousin, Mrs. George.

LOANED BY CAPTAIN F. M. COLSTON

165. Photographs of General Lee and General Joseph E. Johnson.
166. Photograph of General Lee on Traveler.

LOANED BY MRS. HUGHES

167. General Lee's stencil given by him to Mrs. Hughes.
168. Photographs of General and Mrs. Lee colored by Mrs. Lee.

LOANED BY MRS. GENERAL T. J. (STONEWALL) JACKSON

169. Photograph of General Jackson's grave before the removal of his remains to rest under the statue.
170. Photograph of statue in New Orleans erected by Jackson's old soldiers in Metairie Cemetery in 1881.
171. Photograph of monument at Chancellorsville marking the spot where Jackson fell.
172. Photograph of statue of General Jackson in Richmond by Foley. Presented by an English gentleman in 1875.
173. Photograph of Presbyterian Church in Lexington, VA, in which General Jackson worshiped.
174. Photograph of statue of General Jackson at Lexington, VA.
175. Colored photograph of room in Mrs. Jackson's house in which are kept General Jackson's books and personal memorials.
176. Photograph of the monument erected by the U. D. C. at Dallas, TX.
177. Miniature of General Jackson.
178. Miniature of General Jackson's father.
179. General Jackson's watch pocket.
180. Card case containing two cards engraved "Major T. J. Jackson."
181. Paper knife presented to General Jackson by Mexicans.
182. Pipe made by a Confederate soldier while in prison and presented to Jackson.
183. Souvenir spoon.

LOANED BY MR. EUGENE BLACKFORD

184. Leave of absence signed by generals Jackson and Rhodes.
185. Lock of General Jackson's hair.

LOANED BY MR. WILLIAM H. SAXTON.

186. Portrait of General Jackson.

LOANED BY DR. PRESTON

187. Cane of General Jackson's.
188. Early portrait of General Jackson.
189. Letters written from battlefields by General Jackson.

LOANED BY MRS. ROBERT M. COMBS

190. Portrait of General Jackson taken from the home of Thomas Patterson, Esq. Patterson was imprisoned at Fort McHenry. The picture was hung upside down in the Provost Marshal's office until the end of the war.

LOANED BY MRS. WILLIAM McGUIRE

191. Buttons cut from the coat of General Jackson by Dr. McGuire.
192. Flask sent from England to Gen. Jackson and by him given to his aide J. Faulkner.

Loaned by Mr. George Armistead
193. Lock of General Jackson's hair.

Loaned by Mrs. M. M. Brannon
194. Picture of General Jackson's boyhood home.

Loaned by Captain F. M. Colston
195. General Jackson's after photograph by Minnis & Cowell 1863.

Loaned by Mrs. Sara B. Hawks
196. Camp Chair of General Jackson.

Loaned by Captain Augustine J. Smith
197. Piece of doorsill of the room in which General Jackson was born.

Loaned by Mr. Hooper
198. Autographed letter of General Jackson.

Loaned by Major Wilson
199. Autographed letters of generals Jackson and Joseph E. Johnson belonging to the Ashby family.

Loaned by Wells J. Hawks, Esq.
200. Photograph of General Jackson's staff taken in Richmond after his funeral.
201. Camp chair used by General Jackson.

Loaned by Mrs. Arnold Elzy
202. Sword and sash of General Arnold Elzey.

Loaned by Mrs. Winder
203. Sword, uniform, and saddle of General Charles S. Winder.

Loaned by Mrs. Basil Duke
204. Water color portrait of General John H. Morgan.

Loaned by Col. R. C. Morgan
205. Silver spur given General Morgan by ladies of Lynchburg.
206. Pistol given General Morgan by the widow of General Bernard Bee.
207. Ivory martingal ring taken from General Morgan at the time of his capture in Ohio and returned to his brother, Col. R. C. Morgan, after the war.

Loaned by Theodore I. Garnett, Esq.

208. Field glasses of General J. E. B. Stuart presented to his A.D.C. Theodore Garnett on the battlefield of Yellow Tavern by Stuart a short time before receiving his mortal wound.

Loaned by Mrs. George R. Goldsborough

209. Camp candlestick of General Stuart's with a piece of candle as last used.

Loaned by Mrs. Fitzhugh Lee

210. Sword of General Fitzhugh Lee.
211. Headquarters flag of General Fitzhugh Lee made by the ladies of Baltimore and carried to him by Miss Hetty Cary.

Loaned by Captain John D. Smith

212. Fatigue uniform captain of Artillery.
213. Official reports Army of Northern Virginia.
214. English saddle and holsters purchased from Ordnance Bureau, Richmond.
215. Field glasses issued by Ordnance Department to an Artillery captain. One of the barrels was shattered by a musket ball at Hanover Junction May 1864.
216. Confederate States ordnance manual.

Loaned by Miss Aida C. White

217. Sword of Major Harry Gilmor.
218. Picture of Harry Gilmor loaned by his son.

Loaned by Mrs. Robert W. Hunter

219. Pistol found on battlefield of Brandy Station.

Loaned by Mrs. D. Giraud Wright

220. Handkerchief used as a flag of truce. Louis T. Wigfall tied it to his sword when he demanded the surrender of Fort Sumter while acting as an aide to Gen. Beauregard.
221. Portion of flag staff of Fort Sumter shattered by shot during the siege.
222. Colt Army revolver carrier by Senator Wigfall during the siege of Fort Sumter.
223. Sword of Major Francis H. Wigfall used throughout the war.

Loaned by William H. Murry

224. Flag staff from the flag presented by the ladies of Baltimore to Co. A, 2nd Maryland Infantry. Shot in two while on the breastworks at Cold Harbor in 1864.

LOANED BY MRS. JOHN T. MASON

225. Sword sash worn in three wars. War of 1812, Mexican War, and the War Between the States. Worn by Major Thomas Rowland 17th Virginia Infantry.

LOANED BY MR. CHARLES GROGAN

226. Uniform jacket spun, woven, and made in Jefferson County, VA. Stained with blood of the wearer, Lt. Charles Grogan, A.D.C. to Gen. Trimble at Chancellorsville and torn by a shell at Gettysburg.

LOANED BY MISS DORO HOFFMAN

227. Bayonet from Gettysburg battlefield.

LOANED BY MRS. EDGEWORTH BIRD

228. Field glasses of Maj. Gen. John C. Breckinridge used at Shiloh and throughout the war. Given to Mrs. Bird when he disbanded his staff at her home May 7, 1865.
229. Cannon ball that passed through the Henry House at the first battle of Bull Run. Picked up two days later by an officer of the 15th Georgia Regiment and sent to his young son.

LOANED BY MRS. ROBERT ATKINSON

230. Piece of flag sent by Maryland women to their soldiers in the C. S. Army.

LOANED BY MISS KATE M. ROWLAND

231. Uniform coat of Major Thomas Rowland 17th Virginia Infantry. Buttons and insignia of rank were removed at the close of the war.
232. Piece of a Confederate Hospital Flag.
233. Piece of Confederate Flag from Fort Hatteras given by a prisoner to Judge Scott of the Maryland Legislature, then a prisoner at Fort Warren who in turn gave it to Miss Rowland.
234. Piece of shell picked up in the ruins of the Tredegar Iron Works April 2, 1865.
235. Shoulder strap and button of a Confederate surgeon.
236. C. S. Army Regulations.
237. Reports of the Army of Northern Virginia.

LOANED BY KEITH DRAGAN, DARLINGTON, SC

238. Flag of the Pee Dee Light Artillery, McIntosh's Battalion. Carried in Seven Day battles, Second Manassas, Ox Hill, Harpers Ferry, Sharpsburg, Fredericksburg, Chancellorsville, Gettysburg, Wilderness, Spottsylvania, Cold Harbor. E. Keith Dargan was the first Color Bearer.

LOANED BY MRS. MARY S. HUGHES

239. Swords from the battlefield of Kernstown.
240. Small Confederate Flag carried from Manassas to Appomattox.
241. Cartridge box found at Kernstown.
242. Pocketbook from Appomattox with Confederate money.

LOANED BY MRS. FRANCIS T. MILLER

243. Piece of flagstaff from Fort Sumter.
244. Pieces of shells from fortifications around Charleston.

LOANED BY MR. HOWARD

245. Flag of Truce letter from Gen. Ord USA to Lt. Col. James Howard commanding 18th and 20th Virginia artillery battalions, passing Mr. Winder and Miss Smith.

LOANED BY MRS. R. SNOWDEN ANDREWS

246. Shell jacket worn by Col. R. Snowden Andrews while in command of nine batteries of artillery of the Stonewall Division during the battle of Cedar Mountain. During the battle Andrews was struck in the abdomen by a Union artillery round, but some how managed to survive. The jacket shows the effects of this wound.
247. Facsimile of letter in reference to Col. Andrews promotion.

LOANED BY MISS JOHNSON

248. Sash of Major Lucius J. Johnson 17th North Carolina.

LOANED BY EUGENE BLACKFORD, ESQ.

249. Company muster roll of the 5th Alabama Infantry. The first company mustered for the war.
250. Official signatures of generals Rodes and Van Dorn.
251. Provost Marshal's permit.
252. Letter of General Rodes.

LOANED BY MR. FREDERICK H. SMITH

253. Bowie knife from the First Manassas battlefield.
254. Parole of Captain Frederick H. Smith, C. S. Niter and Mining Corps.
255. War Department pass of Captain F. H. Smith.

LOANED BY CAPTAIN WILLIAM I. RASIN

256. Flag presented by the ladies of Kent County Maryland.
257. Sword used by Captain Rasin.
258. Pistols used by Captain Rasin.
259. Sash of Captain Rasin.
260. Photographs of Confederate generals.

261. Photograph of woman who nursed Capt. Rasin when wounded in Pennsylvania.
262. Confederate songs and music.

LOANED BY CAPTAIN R. CURZON HOFFMAN

263. Captain's commission of R. Curzon Hoffman.

LOANED BY F. M. COLSTON, ESQ.

264. Parole of an officer at Appomattox.
265. "The Artillery Duel." Original drawing by Allen C. Redwood.
266. "The Rabbit Hunt in Camp." Original drawing by William L. Sheppard.
267. "The Line of Battle." Original drawing by W. L. Sheppard.

LOANED BY MISS FANNY STEWART

268. Autographed photo of Lt. Gen. A. P. Stewart.

LOANED BY MRS. HUGES

269. Badge worn during the war by Mr. Hagerty, a member of Purcell's Battery, Pegram's Battalion.

LOANED BY MISS CAUGHY

270. Confederate flag with history.

LOANED BY J. WEST ALDRIDGE, ESQ.

271. The Paymaster's box which contained $100,000 taken in the "Greenback Raid."
272. Copy of Mosby's farewell to his men.
273. Pistol of a Confederate killed at Gettysburg.

LOANED BY MRS. J. H. TEGMEYER

274. Framed Confederate currency.

LOANED BY MRS. WILLIAM H. STEWART

275. Flag of Co. B, 6th Virginia retained by its Major, Daniel A. Grimsley.
276. War needle book of Thomas Graham, 1st Virginia Cavalry.
277. Bullets fired at Rev. Samuel S. Lambeth, Chaplain 10th Virginia Infantry.

LOANED BY MRS. WILLIAM MCGUIRE

278. Picture of Dr. William McGuire drawn by a prisoner at Point Lookout.

LOANED BY MISS ISABEL MORDECAI

279. Bullets from forts Wagner and Moultrie, SC.

LOANED BY MISS STUART

280. Cannon ball with letter.
281. Spurs.
282. Mess knife, fork and spoon.
283. Revolver.
284. Carbine made in Richmond.
285. Saber.
286. Officers sash.

LOANED BY MR. B. R. CODWISE

287. Morning Report of the 25th Virginia Infantry.

LOANED BY MRS. CHARLES MARSHALL

288. Commission of two officers.
289. Spurs.

LOANED BY MRS. POST

290. Overcoat of an officer in the Maryland cavalry.

LOANED BY MRS. BRIDGES

291. Relics of Major James Breathed.

LOANED BY MRS. MARIAN C. GAMBRILL

292. Shell that burst near General Taliaferro at Rapidan Station.
293. Jug covered with bullets from different battlefields.

LOANED BY WELLS J. HAWKS

294. Autographed letter of General Jubal Early.
295. Autographed letter of General R. S. Ewell.
296. Autographed letter of General Joseph E. Johnson.
297. Autographed letter of President Jefferson Davis.
298. Autographed letter of General Robert E. Lee.
299. Saber of a "Black Horse" cavalryman.

LOANED BY MRS. THOMAS NELSON

300. Cannon made from the boiler of the C.S.S. *Virginia*.

LOANED BY MRS. JOHN T. MASON

301. Sword worn by Passed Midshipman J. T. Mason on the C. S. S. *Shenandoah*.
302. Barometer captured from a whaler by the *Shenandoah*.
303. Walrus tusk captured by the *Shenandoah*.
304. Scale drawing of the C. S. S. *Shenandoah* by Lt. Dabney.

LOANED BY MISS KATE MASON ROWLAND

305. Naval uniform buttons of Passed Midshipment John T. Mason.
306. Small items made of whale's teeth by sailors of the *Shenandoah*.
307. C. S. Navy Regulations.

LOANED BY MISS FLORENCE MACKUBIN

308. Confederate naval buttons from the uniform of Captain John Taylor Wood.

LOANED BY REV. WILLIAM F. BRAND

309. Banner carried by Lt. Robert Brand when capturing the Federal cruiser Indianola.

LOANED BY MRS. HOBART KEECH

310. Yardstick made of wood from the *Merrimac*.

LOANED BY MISS CAUGHY

311. Photograph of Admiral Semmes.

LOANED BY MRS. GRESHAM

312. Fragments of the *Merrimac*.
313. Confederate States banknote.

LOANED BY MISS KATE MASON ROWLAND

314. State bank notes.
315. Railroad pass Melbourne, Australia, given to Midshipman John T. Mason.
316. Confederate newspaper.

LOANED BY REV. C. RANDOLPH PAGE

317. Confederate Bond, showing the faith of a soldier who took it in exchange for the price of a house.

LOANED BY MISS NANNIE T. FLOYD.

318. Confederate Bond No. 430 for $600, to E. H. Smith. Signed by John N. Hendren.
319. Confederate 4% Bond No. 7809, February 17, 1864. $100 to E. H. Smith.

LOANED BY MISS CHARLOTTE DENNIS

320. Facsimile (in gold) of the seal of the Confederate States.

LOANED BY MRS. ROBERT W. HUNTER

321. Confederate newspaper.

LOANED BY MRS. EUGENE BLACKFORD

322.   Confederate bond and currency.

LOANED BY MS. CHARLES M. PARKMAN

323.   Gold die from which was struck the Seal of the Confederate States.

LOANED BY MRS. HELEN PENDELTON

324.   Silver facsimile of the Seal of the Confederate States.

LOANED BY MRS. WILLIAM MCGUIRE

325.   Picture of Mrs. Jefferson Davis taken during the war.

LOANED BY MISS. C. C. BARNEWLL

326.   Document dated 1698 found on the estate of John E. Barnwell of Beaufort, SC, by an officer in the South Atlantic Blockading Squadron and returned by him.
327.   War letters.

LOANED BY MRS. J. R. MORRISON

328.   Jelly glass given by Col. John S. Mosby to a little girl when he was wounded.

LOANED BY MRS. MCHENRY HOWARD

329.   Jewelry made by prisoners at Johnson's Island for Mrs. Charles Howard.

LOANED BY MRS. D. G. WRIGHT

330.   Confederate song.

LOANED BY L. SPIER

331.   Vicksburg Newspaper issued the day before the surrender July 3, 1863.
332.   Envelope with picture and poem.
333.   Invitation to a banquet given for Hon. Jefferson Davis, June 13, 1857.

LOANED BY MISS DORA HOFFMAN

334.   Jewelry made by Confederate prisoners.

LOANED BY MISS KING

335.   Fan made by a Prisoner of State at Fort McHenry.

LOANED BY MISS KATE MASON ROWLAND

336.   Confederate primer.
337.   Confederate music.
338.   Virginia Secession Cockade—1861.

LOANED BY DR. RUSSELL

339. Mirror used by President Davis while a prisoner at Fortress Monroe.

LOANED BY MISS NANNIE T. FLOYD

340. Letter to W. S. Floyd, Richmond, VA, from Columbia, SC.
341. Letter from W. S. Floyd from a soldier in camp near Richmond.
342. Letter to Thomas T. Smith, Richmond from Northampton County, VA. Sent through the blockade.
343. Horseshoe made of wood from the house where General T. J. Jackson was born.

LOANED BY MRS. ROBERT W. HUNTER

344. Confederate Testament.
345. Hymns for the camp.
346. Confederate letters and passes.
347. Invitation for a ball of Gen. Fitzhugh Lee's Cavalry at Charlottesville 1-20-1864.

LOANED BY DR. PRESTON

348. Autographs of Mrs. Mary Custis Lee.
349. Autograph of Mrs. Margaret J. Preston.
350. Original manuscript of "Beechenbrook."
351. "Breechenbrook" printed on "war paper."

LOANED BY MISS FLORENCE MACKUBIN

352. Pillow cushion made and presented to Hon. Clement C. Clay by the ladies of Baltimore when in prison at Fortress Monroe.

LOANED BY MRS. A. C. SCHAEFER

353. Cotton containing bullets fired into Atlanta during the siege.

LOANED BY MRS. HOLMES CONRAD

354. Scrapbook of war items.

LOANED BY MISS NANNIE T. FLOYD

355. Parole of J. Frederick Floyd that was never broken. He has never voted and is still a paroled prisoner.

LOANED BY MRS. HUGH H. LEE

356. Sock, unfinished when Mrs. Lee was sent under armed escort by General Sheridan from her home in Winchester February 1865.
357. Pen with which was signed the Louisiana Ordinance of Secession.

LOANED BY MISS DORA HOFFMAN

358. Lock of hair from Hon. C. C. Clay of Alabama.
359. Seaweed pressed by Confederate prisoner at Point Lookout.
360. Envelope from Fort Delaware made from wrapping paper.

LOANED BY MRS. FRANCIS T. MILES

361. "The Lost Cause."
362. Confederate currency.
363. South Carolina state currency.

LOANED BY MRS. HOWARD

364. Book of uniforms of the Confederacy.

LOANED BY MRS. RIDGELY

365. Book of autographs of prisoners at Johnson's Island.

LOANED BY MRS. WILLIAM P. MCGUIRE

366. Hymnbook of G. H. Wright 12th North Carolina Regiment. Killed in battle.

LOANED BY MRS. DANIELS

367. Charms made by prisoners at Camp Chase.

LOANED BY MRS. TAYLOR

368. Picture of Major Wilson Presstman C. S. Engineers.

LOANED BY MRS. CHARLES MARSHALL

369. Portrait of Col. Charles Marshall of Gen. Lee's staff by Dabour.

LOANED BY J. SCHAEFFER

370. Jacket of William Quinn 1st Virginia Infantry killed at First Manassas.

LOANED BY MRS. R. B. CHEW

371. Flag of Chew's Battery, Col. R. B. Chew commanding.
372. Last address of Col. Mosby to his men written at Wanland, Fauquier County, VA.

The following items were without provenance and are assumed to be part of the Home's permanent collection.

373. Musket barrel from Cold Harbor battlefield.
374. Battle flag of the 8th Virginia Cavalry
375. Framed picture "Manual of Arms" of the 1st Maryland under fire at Gaines' Mills.

376. Framed picture of the C.S.S. *Alabama* or No. 290.
377. Framed picture of a Confederate Sloop of war taken off Nassau in 1863.
378. Framed parole, furlough and other papers of Lt. F. C. Slingluff Co. F, 1st MD Cav.
379. Framed autographed letter from Stonewall Jackson to Gen. Isaac R. Trimble.
380. Regimental Colors of the 2nd Maryland Infantry,
381. Colors presented to the Frederick Volunteers, Co. A, 1st Maryland Infantry.
382. Drum used by Hosea Pitt, Drum Major 1st Maryland Infantry 1861–1865.
383. Framed picture "Second Relief."
384. Framed picture "After the Battle."
385. Framed picture "Halt."
386. Part of armor of the C.S.S. Ram *Virginia*.
387. Framed Muster Roll and requisitions of the Baltimore Light Artillery.
388. Framed picture of Mosby and his men.
389. Framed picture "Virginia 1864."
390. Sword bayonet.
391. Sword belonging to Capt. H. Steinburg found on Gettysburg battlefield.
392. Sword worn by Col. Ridgely Brown killed commanding 1st Maryland Cavalry.
393. Sword—relic of the war.
394. Framed picture of Camp St. Mary's—Winter Quarters of the Maryland Line near Hanover Junction, January 1864.
395. Framed picture "In Line of Battle Awaiting Orders."
396. Framed picture of prisoners at Fort Warren from the C.S.S. Ironclad *Atlanta* and the Privateer *Tacony* 1863–1864.
397. General Lee's camp chair presented to him by Joshua Thomas.
398. Autograph of Gen. N. B. Forrest.
399. One dollar Confederate note donated by Mrs. Mary A. Deems.
400. Framed Roster of the Third Maryland Artillery.
401. Framed print of the charge of the 2nd Maryland Infantry at Culp's Hill.
402. Framed print of the charge of the 1st Maryland Infantry and the death of Ashby.
403. Shell from the South Mountain Battlefield.
404. Two bullets from Culp's Hill.
405. Spurs worn by John S. Hammond of Baltimore City. 1st Sgt. Co. A, 2nd GA Cav.
406. Cap worn by Lt. Col. Bradley T. Johnson.
407. Field glass used by Gen. Bradley T. Johnson.
408. Kentucky sword belt.
409. Pistol carried by Benjamin H. Sweeting of Harford County, MD.
410. Photograph of General Turner Ashby.

411. Piece of cornerstone of Gen. R .E. Lee's monument at Richmond.
412. Original Muster Roll of Capt. E. R. Dorsey's Co. 1st Maryland Infantry.
413. Photograph of Captain Matthew F. Maury C.S.N.
414. Belt worn during the war.
415. Confederate postage stamps.
416. Field glass of Col. Heros Von Borcke.
417. C. S. Buckle.
418. Shin Plaster issued during the war.
419. $1000 Confederate Bond.
420. Confederate shell from the site of Gen. Meade's monument at Gettysburg.
421. Twenty photographs of Confederate officers.
422. Pass of Henry Briscoe from the Provost Marshal of Baltimore.
423. Paymasters receipt of Dr. Henry Briscoe Surgeon 26th Virginia Infantry.
424. Bullet from the Crater.
425. Confederate cartridges.
426. Tobacco pouch used by Col. Harry Gilmor.
427. Canteen from the Gettysburg battlefield.
428. Flask.
429. Two photographs of General Allen Thomas.
430. Parole of John M. Norvell.
431. Buckle from the cap of General Bee.
432. Confederate Navy button.
433. Three flints issued to Cpl. Eugene H. Brown Co. C, 16th Va Infantry in 1861.
434. Pair of snuffers brought from Corinth, MS, by Lt. E. H. Browne C.S.N.
435. Pistol owned by Major W. L. Bailey.
436. Uniform coat worn by Lt. H. H. Bean Co I, 1st Maryland Infantry.
437. Original Muster Roll of Capt. Augustus F. Schwartze Co. F, 1st MD Cavalry.
438. Requisition of Capt. A. F. Schwartze Co. F, 1st MD Cavalry.
439. Invoice of Stores to Capt. F. A. Bond from Lt. L. Wilcox Brown.
440. Illustrated pack of cards.
441. Blanket belonging to Lt. E. H. Browne C.S.N.
442. Three bullets from the Fredericksburg battlefield.
443. Bullets from the New Market battlefield.
444. Pistol used by Pvt. W. A. Robbins Co. D, 24th Virginia Cavalry.
445. Cap box and cartridge box used during the war.
446. Knapsack Co. F, 3rd North Carolina Regiment.
447. Bayonet and belt used during the war.
448. Haversack used by Captain Augustine J. Smith.
449. Confederate haversack.
450. Cavalry boots worn by General Bradley T. Johnson.
451. Confederate bridle bit.

452. Jacket worn by William H. Harrison Co. A, 2nd Maryland Infantry.
453. Confederate candle or "Taper."
454. Discharge and parole of L. H. Schoolfield Baltimore Light Artillery.
455. Descriptive List of Private W. C. Duncan.
456. Piece of wood cut from a tree at Cold Harbor.
457. Letter from Gen. Munford to Col. Augustus Dorsey 1st Maryland Cavalry.
458. Special Order from Gen. Munford to Col. G. W. Dorsey disbanding the First Maryland Cavalry April 28, 1865.
459. Two CSA notes that were in the pocketbook of Gen. R. E. Lee at the surrender.
460. Pistol and holster used by John Zellers 35th Virginia Cavalry.
461. Match safe used by Col. Ridgely Brown 1st Maryland Cavalry.
462. Drinking cup of Col. Ridgely Brown.
463. Belt found on the Wilderness battlefield.
464. Sock worn during the war.
465. C. S. A. paper from Judah P. Benjamin.
466. Knife blade from Fort Morgan.
467. Color lance head.
468. Muster Roll of Co. K, Captain George R. Gaither.
469. Silver fork from the Officers Mess on the C. S. Gunboat *Chickamauga* used by E. H. Brow.
470. A piece of comb used by William S. Skidmore during the entire war.
471. Hand glass found by W. S. Skidmore and used by him to the end of the war.
472. Book bought from a Sutler by W. S. Skidmore for $8.00.
473. Thirteen pieces of old coin found by W. S. Skidmore on different battle-fields.
474. Ten dollar Confederate note. Part of the last pay received by W. S. Skidmore Co. A, 9th Virginia Cavalry.
475. Collection of relics set in wood from the Gettysburg battlefield.
476. Regimental Colors of the 2nd Maryland Infantry carried by them at Gettysburg and the first planted on Culp's Hill in the works captured by Steuart's Brigade.
477. Walking cane cut from a tree that grew over Stonewall Jackson's grave.
478. Shell found on the Gettysburg battlefield by Hugh McWilliams July 25, 1866.
479. Picture of Confederate officers in their old U. S. Army uniforms.
480. Photograph—members of the Maryland Line Confederate Soldiers' Home and their friends at Pen Mar September 10, 1890.
481. Photograph of Maj. Gen. Isaac R. Trimble.
482. Photograph of Brig. Gen. George H. Steuart.
483. Photograph of Brig. Gen. Lloyd Tilghman.
484. Photograph Commodore George N. Hollins.

485. Photograph of Brig. Gen. Charles S. Winder.
486. Photograph of Huge McWilliams Co. C, 1st Maryland Cavalry.
487. Print—"Burial of Latane."
488. Photograph of F. Nichols Crouch, author of "Kathleen Mavoureen."
489. Memorial picture, Confederate officers.
490. Photograph of General R. E. Lee.
491. Photographic views of the Soldiers' Home.
492. Photograph of Col. Ridgely Brown.
493. Photograph of General Hood's family.
494. Photograph of Gen. James Archer of Harford County, MD.
495. Photograph of Lt. Col. James R. Herbert. Commanded the 2nd Maryland Infantry.
496. Photograph of General Bradley T. Johnson.
497. Photograph of President Davis and his Cabinet.

Where are they now?

APPENDIX C

ROSTER OF UNITED CONFEDERATE VETERANS CAMPS IN THE STATE OF MARYLAND AS OF APRIL 1913

Alexander Young Camp #500, Frederick, MD
Captain W.H. Shipley Commander, Lt. Joseph H. Trundle, Adjutant

Ridgely Brown Camp #518, Gaithersburg, MD
Gen. Spencer C. Jones Commander, Edmund L. Amies, Adjutant

James R. Herbert Camp #657, Baltimore, MD
J.B. Sutherland Commander, Charles H. Mettee Adjutant

Franklin Buchanan Camp #747, Baltimore, MD
Maj. William M. Pegram Commander, Alfred J. McKay Adjutant

George H. Steuart Camp #777, Annapolis, MD
James W. Owens Commander

Charles S. Winder Camp #989, Easton, MD
Gen. Oswald Tilghman Commander, Louis W. Trail Adjutant

James Breathed Camp #1046, Cumberland, MD
James Clark, Acting Commander

Bradley T. Johnson Camp #1110, Leonardtown, MD
Frank V. King Commander

Isaac R. Trimble Camp #1215, Baltimore, MD
William M. Cary Commander

George M. Emack Camp #1471, Hyattsville, MD
John F. Rickey Commander, John W. Williams Adjutant

Arnold Elzey Camp #1515, Baltimore, MD
John McGregor Commander, James W. Denny Adjutant

APPENDIX D

MARYLAND DIVISION SONS OF CONFEDERATE VETERANS AS OF JUNE 2001

Division Commander: Chris Beck

Camps: The Maryland Division of the SCV includes Washington, DC, and the one Camp in the state of New Jersey at this time.

Jefferson Davis Camp #305. Fr. Alister Anderson, Commander

Captain Vincent Camilier Camp #1359. Mr. John Stober, Jr., Commander

Colonel Harry Gilmor Camp #1388. Mr. Barry Klohr, Commander

Colonel William Norris Camp #1398. Mr. Joseph F. Bach, Commander

Private Wallace Bowling Camp #1400. Mr. James B. Dunbar, Commander

Private Meredith Poole Camp #1501. Mr. David J. Carlough, Jr., Commander

Captain James I. Waddell Camp #1608. Mr. Charles Kolodgy, Commander

Maryland Line CSA Camp #1741. Mr. Robert W. Parker, Commander

Private Eli Scott Dance Camp # 1751. Mr. Daniel J. Heacock, Commander

Major General Isaac Ridgeway Trimble Camp #1836. Lt. Col. John P. Zebelean III, USAF (Ret), Commander

Major General Arnold Elzey Camp # 1940. Mr. Jeffrey J. Martin, Commander

APPENDIX E

MARYLAND DIVISION UNITED DAUGHTERS OF THE CONFEDERACY

The following is a table of organization for the Maryland Division listing all known chapters with their name, chapter number, date of organization and current president if not inactive. The information is taken from their 2000–2002 Directory.

President of the Maryland Division: Mary Elizabeth Kerby

Chapters:

Baltimore #8, May 5, 1895. President, Mrs. Virginia H. Sollers- Hoffmaster

Admiral Buchanan #134 Easton – Inactive

Harford #144, April 28, 1898. President, Mrs. Allen E. Edwards

Fitzhugh Lee #279 Frederick, December, 1898. President, Ms. Carol Ann Hobbs

Frank A. Bond #370 Jessup – Inactive

Cecil Chapter #478 Chesapeake City – Inactive

Ridgely Brown #1349 Rockville – Inactive

Co. A, First Maryland Cavalry #1858 Ellicott City, September 12, 1924. President, Mrs. James F. Keenan

James R. Wheeler #1859 Baltimore, September 24, 1924. Mrs. Donald W. Downey

E.V. White #1360 Poolesville – Inactive

John F. Hickey #1677 Hyattsville – Inactive

Henry Kyd Douglas #1720 Hagerstown – Inactive

Gen. Bradley T. Johnson #1940 Baltimore, June 4, 1927. President, Miss Nancy F. Delea

W. H. Murray #1944 Annapolis, March 18, 1927. President, Mrs. T. Patrick Robertson

General Robert E. Lee #2043 Baltimore – Inactive

Andrew Jackson Gwynn #2059 Upper Marlboro – Inactive

Stonewall Jackson #2062 Baltimore – Inactive

Col. William Rison #2063 Baltimore – Inactive

Jefferson Davis #2168 Boonsboro – Inactive

CSS *Shenandoah* #2328 Annapolis – Inactive

Col. Richard Thomas Zarvona #2571 Charlotte Hall, March 12, 1992. Mrs. Louis Purnell

Jane Margaret Cary Baltimore – never chartered

NOTES

Chapter One Notes

1. Paul J. Travers, *The Patapsco, Baltimore's River of History*. (Tidewater Publishers: 1990), pp. 24-28.
2. Beryl Frank, *A Pictorial History of Pikesville, Maryland*, Baltimore County Public Library: 1982, p. 1-5.
3. Ibid, pp. 6-7.
4. *Illustrated Souvenir of the Maryland Line Confederate Soldiers Home*. Compiled by Captain George W. Booth. (Maryland Line Confederate Soldiers' Home: 1894), p. 8. Here after referred to as Booth.
5. Booth, p. 8; Frank, pp. 6-7.

Chapter 2 Notes

1. Charles L. Shipley, *The Old Confederate Soldiers' Home*, (No Publisher: 1944), p. 8.
2. Booth, pp. 12-14.
3. Maryland Historical Trust Inventory Form for State Historic Sites Survey. Description item 7 and 8, Shipley, p. 24.
4. Shipley, pp. 4-5.
5. Francis B. Heitman, *Historical Register and Dictionary of the United States Army*, (GPO: 1903), Vol. I, p. 699; Original letter in the collection of Mr. Gil Barrett; Roger D. Hunt, *Brevet Brigadier Generals in Blue*, (Olde Soldier Books:1990), p. 387.
6. Ezra J. Warner, *Generals in Blue*, (LSU Press: 1964), p. 446; Shipley, p. 14.
7. Mary Jane Kline, *St. Borromeo Parish*, (St. Charles Borromeo Parish: 1998), pp. 22-23.
8. Jeffrey L. Rhoades, *Scapegoat General The Story of Major General Benjamin Huger, CSA*, (Arcbon Book: 1985), pp. 1-3.
9. Ibid, pp. 5,7.
10. Ibid, pp. 11, 16-17.
11. Ibid, pp. 27-28; Warner, p. 144.
12. Shipley, p. 12.
13. *History and Roster of Maryland Volunteers, War 1861-5*, (The General Assembly of MD: 1898), Vol. I p. 460.
14. Shipley, p. 15.

15. W.W. Goldsborough, *The Maryland Line in the Confederate Army 1861-1865*, (Kennikat Press: 1972), p. 158; Shipley, p. 16.

Chapter 3 Notes

1. Booth, pp. 11-12.
2. Ibid, pp. 12, 97.
3. Thornton W. Cox, "I Remember The Old Men In Faded Gray," *Baltimore Sun* August 9, 1953.
4. Booth, p. 14.
5. First Annual Report issued by the Board of Managers of the Maryland Line Confederate Soldiers' Home, pp. 4-9.
6. Shipley, p. 17.
7. Booth, pp. 19-52.
8. Shipley, p. 22.
9. Booth, p. 53.
10. Cox; Shipley, p. 17; First Annual Report, p. 11; Lee McCardell, "Mrs. Tunis Surrenders Arsenal To Col. Hobbs," *Baltimore Sun* April 29, 1938.
11. 1899 Announcement of Tournament; 1899 Program of Tournament; Shipley, p. 24.
12. *Baltimore Sun*, June 7, 1910, "Confederate Veterans At Comrades Graves."
13. Frank, p. 31.
14. Shipley, p. 21; Samuel E. Miller, "Confederate Hill, Loudon Park Cemetery, Baltimore, Maryland," (Private Publication: 1962), p. 31.
15. Shipley, p. 22; McCardell.
16. Ibid, pp. 25-26.
17. "A brief History of the Headquarters of the Maryland State Police," (Pikesville, no date); Maryland Historic Trust, Inventory Form for State Historic Sites Survey, Headquarters, Maryland State Police.

Chapter 4 Notes

1. Maryland Historical Society, Maryland Line Confederate Soldiers' Home Record Books, 1882-1932, MS 256, Warner, pp.225-226.
2. MS 256.
3. Letter to General L.L. Lomax outlining requirements for acceptance to the Maryland Line Confederate Soldiers' Home, author's collection.
4. Sample questionnaire, author's collection.
5. "Biographical Sketches of the Members of Maryland Line Confederate Soldiers' Home January 1900," original copy in author's collection.

Chapter 5 Notes

1. Constitution of the Society of the Army and Navy of the Confederate States in the State of Maryland.

2. Booth, pp. 96-97.
3. Joseph M. Balkoski, *The Maryland National Guard. A History of Maryland's Military Forces 1634-1991*. (MNG: 1991), pp. 5-7.
4. Booth, p. 54.
5. Patricia L. Faust Ed. *Historical Times Illustrated Encyclopedia of the Civil War*. (Historical Times: 1986), p. 273; List of Organized Camps of the United Confederate Veterans. (UCV: 1921), p. 1.
6. Original United Confederate Veterans documents in the collection of the author.
7. *Encyclopedia Civil War*, p. 773.
8. Booth, p. 28; Soderberg, p. 29.
9. "What is the Sons of Confederate Veterans." Information bulletin published by the SCV, Hattiesburg, MS.

Chapter 6 Notes

1. First Annual Report of the Ladies Southern Relief Association of Maryland: September 1, 1866; Mable Jones Tracy, *Confederate Monuments in the Monumental City to the War Between the States*, (Gen. B.T. Johnson Chapter #1940 UDC: 1987), p. 16.
2. Ruth Jennings Lawton, Chairman, *The History of the United Daughters of the Confederacy 1894 – 1955*.(U.D.C.: 1955) Vol, I, p. 9.
3. Ibid, p. 12.
4. Ibid, p. 23.
5. Ibid, p. 22.
6. Ibid, pp. 147-149.
7. Ibid, pp. 215-217; *Evening Capitol* (Annapolis), April 21, 1954, "Doctor Given Cross At UDC Convention"; *Maryland Gazette* (Annapolis), April 22, 1954, "State UDC Meeting to be Conducted at West River"; Susan Cooke Soderberg *Lest We Forget*, (White Maine: 1955), pp. 9-11.
8. Tracy, p. 9; Soderberg, pp. 9-11.
9. Tracy, p. 3; Soderberg, pp. 7-8.
10. Pamphlet given out by the UDC to visitors of the Confederate Room. (NP: ND).
11. *The Evening Sun*, June 5, 1952, "UDC Restores 205 Grave Markers of Confederate War Veterans."
12. Lawton, pp. 181-182, 186.
13. *The Evening Sun*, June 5, 1952.

Chapter 7 Notes

1. *Baltimore Sun*, August 15, 1925, "Home for Confederate Women Will Move to Govans."
2. Souvenir Program "Memories of the South," p. 2. Program from a benefit performance at Albaugh's Theatre May 15, 1913. Hereafter referred to as Program.

3. Tracy, p. 23: Soderberg, p. 35.
4. Mrs. Michael K. Williams, "Maryland's Adopted Son of the Confederacy," *United Daughters of the Confederacy Magazine*, April 1987, Vol. XL, Number 4.
5. Program, p. 5; *The Sun*, February 3, 1925, "Widows of Confederate Veterans not to loose Linden Avenue Home."
6. *The Sun*, January 30, 1925, "Confederate Widows Home Passes to Hands of Others."
7. *The Sun*, September 11, 1925, "Six Octogenarians Vacate Linden Avenue House Occupied Since 1906."

Chapter 8 Notes
1. Booth, p. 96.
2. *The Sun*, June 2, 1881, "Confederate Memorial Day."
3. *The Sun*, June 7, 1910, "Confederate Veterans at Comrades Graves."
4. *The Sun*, December 10, 1928, "Members of Confederate Home Board Beginning to Feel Age."
5. *The Sun*, June 6, 1928, "Confederate Dead Will Be Honored."

INDEX